STUFFED

Publications International, Ltd.

Pictured on the front cover: Shortcut Potato and Cheese Pierogi *(page 62).*

Pictured on the back cover *(clockwise from right):* Bacon S'more Bundles *(page 182),* Chicken Fajita Roll-Ups *(page 90)* and Taco Stuffed Cups *(page 36).*

ISBN: 978-1-64558-012-6

Manufactured in China.

8 7 6 5 4 3 2 1

Microwave Cooking: Microwave ovens vary in wattage. Use the cooking times as guidelines and check for doneness before adding more time.

Let's get social!

 @Publications_International

@PublicationsInternational

www.pilcookbooks.com

CONTENTS

BREAKFAST

CHEESE STUFFED BISCUIT BITES

⅓ cup milk

1 tablespoon dried chives

1 teaspoon minced fresh dill weed

½ teaspoon sugar

1 cup biscuit baking mix

1 tablespoon cold butter, cut into thin slices

12 cubes (½ inch) sharp Cheddar cheese, well chilled

1. Preheat oven to 400°F. Line baking sheet with parchment paper or spray with nonstick cooking spray.

2. Combine milk, chives, dill weed and sugar in small bowl; mix well. Let stand 5 minutes. Place biscuit mix in medium bowl. Cut in butter with pastry blender or two knives until mixture resembles coarse crumbs. Add milk mixture; stir gently to form soft sticky dough.

3. Divide dough into 12 walnut-sized balls. Gently press one cheese cube into each ball; pull dough up and around cheese, completely enclosing cheese. Pinch edges to seal. Place on prepared baking sheet.

4. Bake 12 to 14 minutes or until golden brown. Remove to wire rack to cool slightly. Serve warm.

MAKES 12 BISCUITS

DENVER SCRAMBLE FILLED HASH BROWN CUPS

3 tablespoons butter, divided

1 package (20 ounces) refrigerated hash brown potatoes

1½ teaspoons salt, divided

6 eggs

2 tablespoons milk

⅛ teaspoon black pepper

⅛ teaspoon hot pepper sauce or to taste

½ cup diced onion

½ cup diced green bell pepper

½ cup diced ham

⅓ cup shredded Monterey Jack cheese

1. Preheat oven to 400°F. Spray 12 standard (2½-inch) muffin cups with nonstick cooking spray.

2. Melt 2 tablespoons butter. Combine melted butter, potatoes and 1 teaspoon salt in large bowl; toss to coat. Press potatoes into bottoms and up sides of prepared cups (5 to 6 tablespoons per cup).

3. Bake about 35 minutes or until bottoms and sides are golden brown. (Insides of cups will not brown.)

4. When hash brown cups have baked 15 minutes, beat eggs, milk, remaining ½ teaspoon salt, black pepper and hot pepper sauce in medium bowl until well blended. Melt remaining 1 tablespoon butter in large skillet over medium-high heat. Add onion; cook and stir about 4 minutes or until softened. Add bell pepper; cook and stir 4 minutes. Add ham; cook and stir 5 minutes or until bell pepper is crisp-tender. Pour egg mixture into skillet; cook 20 to 30 seconds without stirring or just until edges are beginning to set. Stir around edges and across bottom of skillet with heatproof spatula, forming large curds. Cook 3 to 4 minutes or until eggs are fluffy and barely set, stirring gently.

5. Remove hash brown cups from pan. Fill cups with scrambled egg mixture (about ¼ cup egg mixture per cup); sprinkle with cheese.

MAKES 12 CUPS (4 TO 6 SERVINGS)

CHOCOLATE STUFFED DOUGHNUTS

½ **cup semisweet chocolate chips**

2 **tablespoons whipping cream**

1 **package (7½ ounces) refrigerated buttermilk biscuits (10 biscuits)**

½ **cup granulated or powdered sugar**

¾ **cup vegetable oil**

1. Combine chocolate chips and cream in small microwavable bowl; microwave on HIGH 20 seconds; stir until smooth. Microwave at additional 15-second intervals, if necessary, until chocolate is melted and mixture is smooth. Cover and refrigerate 1 hour or until solid.

2. Separate biscuits. Using melon baller or small teaspoon, scoop out 1 rounded teaspoon chocolate mixture; place in center of each biscuit. Press dough up and around chocolate; pinch to form a ball. Roll pinched end on work surface to seal dough and flatten ball slightly.

3. Place sugar in shallow dish. Heat oil in medium skillet until hot but not smoking. Cook doughnuts in small batches about 30 seconds per side or until golden brown. Drain on paper towel-lined plate.

4. Roll warm doughnuts in sugar to coat. Serve warm or at room temperature. (Doughnuts are best eaten within a few hours of cooking.)

MAKES 10 DOUGHNUTS

TIP: For a quicker chocolate filling, use chocolate chips instead of the chocolate-cream mixture. Place 6 to 8 chips in the center of each biscuit; proceed with shaping and cooking doughnuts as directed.

MEXICAN BREAKFAST BURRITO

8 eggs

¼ teaspoon salt

⅛ teaspoon black pepper

1 tablespoon butter

½ cup canned black beans, rinsed and drained

2 tablespoons sliced green onions

2 (10-inch) flour tortillas

¼ cup (1 ounce) shredded Cheddar cheese

¼ cup salsa

1. Whisk eggs, salt and pepper in medium bowl until well blended. Melt butter in large nonstick skillet over medium heat. Pour egg mixture into skillet; Reduce heat to low; cook just until eggs begin to set, stirring occasionally. Add beans and green onions; cook and stir 3 minutes or just until eggs are cooked through.

2. Spoon egg mixture evenly down centers of tortillas; sprinkle with cheese. Roll up to enclose filling. Cut in half; top with salsa.

MAKES 4 SERVINGS

APPLE BUTTER ROLLS

1 **package (11 ounces) refrigerated breadstick dough (12 breadsticks)**

2 **tablespoons apple butter**

1 **to 1½ teaspoons orange juice**

¼ **cup sifted powdered sugar**

¼ **teaspoon grated orange peel (optional)**

1. Preheat oven to 350°F. Line baking sheet with parchment paper or spray with nonstick cooking spray.

2. Unroll breadstick dough on work surface; separate into 12 pieces along perforations. Gently stretch each piece to 9 inches in length. Twist ends of each piece in opposite directions three or four times. Coil each twisted strip into snail shape on prepared baking sheet; tuck ends underneath. Use thumb to make small indentation in center of each breadstick coil. Spoon about ½ teaspoon apple butter into each indentation.

3. Bake 11 to 13 minutes or until golden brown. Remove to wire rack to cool 10 minutes.

4. Meanwhile, stir 1 teaspoon orange juice into powdered sugar in small bowl until smooth. Add additional orange juice, if necessary, to make pourable glaze. Stir in orange peel, if desired. Drizzle glaze over rolls. Serve warm.

MAKES 12 ROLLS

ASPARAGUS FRITTATA STUFFED PROSCIUTTO CUPS

1 tablespoon olive oil

1 small red onion, finely chopped

1½ cups sliced asparagus (½-inch pieces)

1 clove garlic, minced

12 thin slices prosciutto

8 eggs

½ cup (2 ounces) grated white Cheddar cheese

¼ cup grated Parmesan cheese

2 tablespoons milk

⅛ teaspoon black pepper

1. Preheat oven to 375°F. Spray 12 standard (2½-inch) muffin cups with nonstick cooking spray.

2. Heat oil in large skillet over medium heat. Add onion; cook and stir 4 minutes or until softened. Add asparagus and garlic; cook and stir 8 minutes or until asparagus is crisp-tender. Set aside to cool slightly.

3. Line each prepared muffin cup with prosciutto slice. (Prosciutto should cover cup as much as possible, with edges extending above muffin pan.) Whisk eggs, Cheddar, Parmesan, milk and pepper in large bowl until well blended. Stir in asparagus mixture until blended. Pour into prosciutto-lined cups, filling about three-fourths full.

4. Bake about 20 minutes or until frittatas are puffed and golden brown and edges are pulling away from pan. Cool in pan 10 minutes; remove to wire rack. Serve warm or at room temperature.

MAKES 12 CUPS (6 SERVINGS)

RASPBERRY STUFFED DANISH

1 package (8 ounces) refrigerated crescent roll dough

8 teaspoons raspberry preserves

1 ounce white chocolate, chopped

1. Preheat oven to 375°F. Line baking sheet with parchment paper or spray with nonstick cooking spray.

2. Unroll crescent dough on work surface; separate into eight triangles. Place 1 teaspoon preserves in center of each triangle. Fold right and left corners of long side over filling to top corner to form rectangle. Pinch edges to seal. Place seam side up on prepared baking sheet.

3. Bake 12 minutes or until lightly browned. Remove to wire rack to cool 5 minutes.

4. Place white chocolate in small resealable food storage bag. Microwave on MEDIUM (50%) 1 minute; gently knead bag. Microwave and knead at additional 30-second intervals until chocolate is completely melted. Cut off small corner of bag; drizzle chocolate over Danish.

MAKES 8 DANISH

SPINACH ARTICHOKE EGG SOUFFLÉS

1 package (about 17 ounces) frozen puff pastry (2 sheets), thawed

1 teaspoon olive oil

¼ cup chopped onion

1 clove garlic, minced

¼ cup finely chopped roasted red pepper (1 pepper)

¼ cup finely chopped canned artichoke hearts (about 2 medium)

¼ cup thawed frozen spinach, squeezed dry

3 eggs, separated

½ (8-ounce) package cream cheese, softened

½ teaspoon salt

⅛ teaspoon black pepper

4 tablespoons grated Romano cheese, divided

1. Preheat oven to 400°F. Spray eight 4-inch or 1-cup ramekins or jumbo (3½-inch) muffin pan cups with nonstick cooking spray. Unfold puff pastry; cut each sheet into quarters. Gently press each pastry square into bottoms and partially up sides of prepared ramekins. (Pastry should not reach tops of ramekins.) Place ramekins on baking sheet; refrigerate while preparing filling.

2. Heat oil in medium skillet over medium heat. Add onion; cook and stir 3 minutes or until softened and lightly browned. Add garlic; cook and stir 30 seconds. Add roasted pepper, artichokes and spinach; cook and stir 2 minutes or until all liquid has evaporated.

3. Whisk egg yolks, cream cheese, salt and black pepper in medium bowl until well blended. Stir in vegetable mixture and 3 tablespoons Romano cheese.

4. Beat egg whites in large bowl with electric mixer at high speed 3 minutes or until stiff peaks form. Fold into vegetable mixture until blended. Divide mixture evenly among pastry-lined ramekins; sprinkle with remaining 1 tablespoon Romano cheese. Fold corners of pastry towards center.

5. Bake 25 minutes or until pastry is golden brown and filling is puffed. Cool in ramekins 2 minutes; remove to wire rack. Serve warm.

MAKES 8 SERVINGS

QUICK JELLY STUFFED DOUGHNUTS

Vegetable oil for frying

⅓ **cup coarse sugar**

1 **package (7½ ounces) refrigerated biscuits (10 biscuits)**

1 **cup strawberry preserves***

*If preserves are very chunky, process in food processor 10 seconds or press through fine-mesh sieve.

1. Pour about 2 inches of oil into large heavy saucepan or Dutch oven; clip deep-fry or candy thermometer to side of saucepan. Heat over medium-high heat to 360° to 370°F. Place sugar in shallow dish.

2. Separate biscuits. Fry biscuits in batches 1 minute per side or until puffed and golden brown. Remove to wire rack; immediately roll in sugar to coat.

3. Fit piping bag with medium star tip; fill bag with preserves. Poke hole in side of each doughnut with paring knife; fill with preserves. Serve immediately.

MAKES 10 DOUGHNUTS

RAMEN EGG CUPS

Foil

1 package (3 ounces) chicken-
flavored ramen noodles

6 eggs

2 tablespoons milk

Salt and black pepper

Chopped fresh parsley (optional)

1. Preheat oven to 400°F. Crumble 6 pieces of foil into balls about half the size of standard (2½-inch) muffin cups. Spray 6 muffin cups and foil balls with nonstick cooking spray.

2. Fill medium saucepan half full with water; add ramen seasoning packet and bring to a boil over high heat. Add noodles; cook 1 minute to soften. Rinse and drain under cool running water.

3. Divide noodles among prepared muffin cups, pressing into bottoms and up sides of cups. Place foil ball in each cup to help set shape.

4. Bake 15 minutes. Remove foil balls; return to oven and bake 10 minutes. Cool in pan 5 minutes. *Reduce oven temperature to 325°F.*

5. Carefully crack 1 egg into each noodle cup. Top each egg with 1 teaspoon milk; season with salt and pepper. Bake 10 to 12 minutes until egg whites are completely set and yolks are thickened but not hard. Sprinkle with parsley, if desired. Serve warm.

MAKES 6 SERVINGS

MINI FRUIT STUFFED COFFEECAKES

1 **package (about 17 ounces) frozen puff pastry (2 sheets), thawed**

1 **package (8 ounces) cream cheese, softened**

1 **egg**

2 **tablespoons granulated sugar**

¼ **cup desired fruit filling (apricot jam, strawberry jam, lemon curd or a combination)**

2 **teaspoons milk (optional)**

½ **cup powdered sugar (optional)**

1. Preheat oven to 350°F. Spray 12 standard (2½-inch) muffin cups with nonstick cooking spray.

2. Unroll puff pastry on work surface; cut each sheet into six rectangles. Fit pastry into prepared muffin cups, pressing into bottoms and up sides of cups. (Two sides of each rectangle will extend up over top of muffin pan.)

3. Beat cream cheese in large bowl with electric mixer at medium-high speed until smooth. Add egg and granulated sugar; beat until well blended. Spoon heaping tablespoon cream cheese mixture into each cup; top with 1 teaspoon fruit filling. Snip center of each overhanging pastry with scissors or paring knife; fold resulting four flaps in over filling, overlapping slightly (as you would fold a box).

4. Bake 20 minutes or until pastry is golden brown and filling is set and puffed. Cool in pan 2 minutes; remove to wire rack to cool slightly.

5. Meanwhile, prepare glaze, if desired. Stir milk into powdered sugar in small bowl until smooth. Drizzle over coffeecakes.

MAKES 12 COFFEECAKES

SCRAMBLED EGG STUFFED QUESADILLAS

4 eggs
2 tablespoons milk
4 teaspoons vegetable oil, divided
1 can (4 ounces) chopped mild
   green chiles

8 soft corn tortillas
½ cup (2 ounces) shredded sharp
   Cheddar cheese
¼ cup chopped fresh cilantro
1 ounce pepperoni slices, quartered

1. Whisk eggs and milk in small bowl until well blended. Heat 2 teaspoons oil in large nonstick skillet over medium heat. Add egg mixture; cook just until eggs are set, lifting edges to allow uncooked portion to flow underneath. Remove to plate. Wipe out skillet with paper towel.

2. Spread 1 tablespoon chiles on half of each tortilla. Top with eggs, cheese and cilantro; sprinkle with pepperoni. Fold tortillas in half over filling.

3. Heat remaining 2 teaspoons oil in same skillet over medium heat. Cook quesadillas in two batches 3 minutes per side or until cheese is melted.

MAKES 4 SERVINGS

APPETIZERS

PEPPERONI STUFFED MUSHROOMS

16 medium mushrooms

1 tablespoon olive oil

½ cup finely chopped onion

2 ounces pepperoni, finely chopped (about ½ cup)

¼ cup finely chopped green bell pepper

½ teaspoon seasoned salt

¼ teaspoon dried oregano

⅛ teaspoon black pepper

½ cup crushed buttery crackers (about 12)

¼ cup grated Parmesan cheese

1 tablespoon chopped fresh parsley, plus additional for garnish

1. Preheat oven to 350°F. Line baking sheet with foil; spray foil with nonstick cooking spray.

2. Clean mushrooms; remove stems and set aside caps. Finely chop stems.

3. Heat oil in large skillet over medium-high heat. Add onion; cook and stir 2 to 3 minutes or until softened. Add mushroom stems, pepperoni, bell pepper, seasoned salt, oregano and black pepper; cook and stir about 5 minutes or until vegetables are tender but not browned.

4. Remove from heat; stir in crushed crackers, cheese and 1 tablespoon parsley until blended. Spoon mixture into mushroom caps, mounding slightly in centers. Place filled caps on prepared baking sheet.

5. Bake about 20 minutes or until heated through. Garnish with additional parsley.

MAKES 4 TO 6 SERVINGS

CRAB RANGOON WITH SPICY DIPPING SAUCE

DIPPING SAUCE
- 1 cup ketchup
- ¼ cup chili garlic sauce
- 4 teaspoons Chinese hot mustard

CRAB RANGOON
- 1 package (8 ounces) cream cheese, softened
- 1 can (6 ounces) lump crabmeat, well drained
- ⅓ cup minced green onions
- 1 package (12 ounces) square wonton wrappers
- 1 egg white, beaten
- Vegetable oil for frying

1. For sauce, combine ketchup, chili garlic sauce and mustard in small bowl; mix well.

2. Beat cream cheese in medium bowl with electric mixer at medium speed until light and fluffy. Stir in crabmeat and green onions until well blended.

3. Arrange wonton wrappers, one at a time, on clean work surface. Place 1 rounded teaspoon crab mixture in center of wrapper. Brush inside edges of wonton wrapper with egg white. Fold wonton diagonally in half to form triangle; press edges firmly to seal.

4. Pour oil into large saucepan to depth of 2 inches; heat to 350°F over medium-high heat. Fry wontons in batches 2 minutes per side or until golden brown. Remove to paper towel-lined plate with slotted spoon. Serve immediately with sauce.

MAKES ABOUT 12 SERVINGS (44 WONTONS)

VARIATION: Crab Rangoon can be baked instead of fried, but the results will not be as crisp or as golden in color. Prepare as directed through step 3, then arrange triangles 1 inch apart on parchment-lined baking sheets. Spray tops of triangles with nonstick cooking spray. Bake in preheated 375°F oven about 11 minutes or until lightly browned. Serve immediately.

GOAT CHEESE STUFFED FIGS

7 **fresh firm ripe figs**
7 **slices prosciutto**

1 **package (4 ounces) goat cheese**
Ground black pepper

1. Preheat broiler. Line baking sheet or broiler pan with foil. Cut figs in half vertically. Cut prosciutto slices in half lengthwise to create 14 pieces (about 4 inches long and 1 inch wide).

2. Spread 1 teaspoon goat cheese onto cut side of each fig half. Wrap prosciutto slice around fig and goat cheese. Sprinkle with pepper.

3. Broil about 4 minutes or until cheese softens and figs are heated through.

MAKES 7 SERVINGS

SHRIMP AND CHILE EMPANADAS

DOUGH

- 4 ounces cream cheese, softened
- ½ cup (1 stick) butter, softened
- ¼ cup grated Parmesan cheese
- ½ teaspoon dried oregano
- ¼ teaspoon black pepper
- 1 to 1¼ cups all-purpose flour

SHRIMP FILLING

- 8 ounces cooked peeled shrimp
- 1 can (4 ounces) diced green chiles
- ¼ cup grated Parmesan cheese
- 2 green onions, chopped
- 3 tablespoons chopped fresh cilantro

1. For dough, combine cream cheese, butter, ¼ cup Parmesan, oregano and pepper in food processor; process until smooth. Add 1 cup flour; process until mixture forms dough that leaves side of bowl. (Add additional flour if dough is too sticky.) Shape dough into two balls; cover with plastic wrap and refrigerate 30 minutes or until firm.

2. For filling, combine shrimp, chiles, ¼ cup Parmesan, green onions and cilantro in food processor; process until finely chopped.

3. Preheat oven to 450°F. Place one ball of dough on lightly floured surface; flatten slightly. Knead 5 minutes or until smooth and elastic.

4. Roll out dough to ⅛-inch thickness. Cut out 3-inch circles with biscuit cutter. Gather scraps into a ball; roll out and cut circles to make about 36 rounds total. Place 1 teaspoon filling on each round. Fold dough in half over filling; seal edges with fork. Place on ungreased baking sheets.

5. Bake 10 minutes or until golden brown. Cool slightly on wire rack; serve warm.

MAKES ABOUT 36 EMPANADAS

TACO STUFFED CUPS

1 tablespoon vegetable oil

½ cup chopped onion

½ pound ground turkey or ground beef

1 clove garlic, minced

½ teaspoon dried oregano

½ teaspoon chili powder or taco seasoning mix

¼ teaspoon salt

1¼ cups (5 ounces) shredded taco cheese or Mexican cheese blend, divided

1 package (about 11 ounces) refrigerated breadstick dough

Chopped fresh tomato and sliced green onion (optional)

1. Heat oil in large skillet over medium heat. Add onion; cook until tender. Add turkey; cook and stir until turkey is no longer pink. Stir in garlic, oregano, chili powder and salt. Remove from heat; stir in ½ cup cheese.

2. Preheat oven to 375°F. Lightly spray 24 mini (1¾-inch) muffin cups with nonstick cooking spray.

3. Remove dough from container but do not unroll dough. Separate dough into eight pieces at perforations. Divide each piece into three pieces; roll or pat each piece into 3-inch circle. Press circles into prepared muffin cups. Fill each cup with 1½ to 2 teaspoons turkey mixture.

4. Bake 10 minutes. Sprinkle tops of cups with remaining ¾ cup cheese; bake 2 to 3 minutes or until cheese is melted. Garnish with tomato and green onion.

MAKES 24 CUPS

GUACAMOLE BITES

2 tablespoons vegetable oil

1¼ teaspoons salt, divided

½ teaspoon garlic powder

12 (6-inch) corn tortillas

2 small ripe avocados

2 tablespoons finely chopped onion

1 tablespoon chopped fresh cilantro

2 teaspoons lime juice

1 teaspoon finely chopped jalapeño pepper* or ¼ teaspoon hot pepper sauce

Jalapeño peppers can sting and irritate the skin, so wear rubber gloves when handling peppers and do not touch your eyes.

1. Preheat oven to 375°F. Combine oil, ¾ teaspoon salt and garlic powder in small bowl; mix well.

2. Use biscuit cutter to cut out two 3-inch circles from each tortilla to create 24 circles total. Wrap stack of tortilla circles loosely in waxed paper; microwave on HIGH 10 to 15 seconds or just until softened. Brush one side of each tortilla very lightly with oil mixture; press into 24 mini (1¾-inch) muffin cups, oiled side up. (Do not spray muffin cups with nonstick cooking spray.)

3. Bake about 8 minutes or until crisp. Remove to wire racks to cool.

4. Meanwhile, prepare guacamole. Cut avocados into halves; remove pits. Scoop pulp into large bowl; mash roughly, leaving avocado slightly chunky. Stir in onion, cilantro, lime juice, remaining ½ teaspoon salt and jalapeño; mix well.

5. Fill each tortilla cup with 2 to 3 teaspoons guacamole.

MAKES 12 SERVINGS (24 CUPS)

SAUSAGE ROLLS

8 ounces ground pork

¼ cup finely chopped onion

½ teaspoon coarse salt

1 teaspoon minced garlic

½ teaspoon dried thyme

½ teaspoon dried basil

¼ teaspoon dried marjoram

¼ teaspoon black pepper

1 sheet frozen puff pastry (half of 17-ounce package), thawed

1 egg, beaten

1. Preheat oven to 400°F. Line baking sheet with parchment paper.

2. Combine pork, onion, salt, garlic, thyme, basil, marjoram and pepper in medium bowl; mix well.

3. Place puff pastry on floured surface; cut lengthwise into three strips at seams. Roll each third into 10×4½-inch rectangle. Shape one third of pork mixture into 10-inch log; arrange log along top edge of one pastry rectangle. Brush bottom ½ inch of rectangle with egg. Roll pastry down around pork; press to seal. Cut each roll crosswise into four pieces; place seam side down on prepared baking sheet. Repeat with remaining puff pastry and pork mixture. Brush top of each roll with egg.

4. Bake about 25 minutes or until sausage is cooked through and pastry is golden brown and puffed. Remove to wire rack to cool 10 minutes. Serve warm.

MAKES 4 SERVINGS (12 ROLLS)

SPINACH AND ARTICHOKE STUFFED PARTY CUPS

36 (3-inch) wonton wrappers

1 jar (about 6 ounces) marinated artichoke hearts, drained and chopped

½ (10-ounce) package frozen chopped spinach, thawed and squeezed dry

1 cup (4 ounces) shredded Monterey Jack cheese

½ cup grated Parmesan cheese

½ cup mayonnaise

1 clove garlic, minced

1. Preheat oven to 300°F. Spray 36 mini (1¾-inch) muffin cups with nonstick cooking spray.

2. Press wonton wrappers into prepared muffin cups; spray with cooking spray. Bake 9 minutes or until light golden brown. Carefully remove to wire racks to cool completely.

3. Combine artichokes, spinach, Monterey Jack, Parmesan, mayonnaise and garlic in medium bowl; mix well. Fill each wonton cup with about 1½ teaspoons spinach-artichoke mixture. Place on baking sheets.

4. Bake 7 minutes or until heated through. Serve immediately.

MAKES 36 CUPS

TIP: If you have leftover spinach-artichoke mixture after filling the wonton cups, place the mixture in a shallow ovenproof dish and bake it at 350°F until hot and bubbly. Serve it with bread or crackers as a dip.

CRAB STUFFED TOMATOES

16 large cherry tomatoes (about 1½ inches in diameter)

3 tablespoons mayonnaise

1 small clove garlic, minced

½ teaspoon lemon juice

¾ cup fresh or refrigerated canned crabmeat*

3 tablespoons chopped pimiento-stuffed green olives

2 tablespoons slivered almonds or pinenuts

⅛ teaspoon black pepper

Choose special grade crabmeat for this recipe. It is less expensive and already flaked but just as flavorful as backfin, lump or claw meat. Look for it in the refrigerated seafood section of the supermarket. Shelf-stable canned crabmeat can be substituted.

1. Cut small slice from bottoms of cherry tomatoes so they stand upright. Cut off top of tomatoes; scoop out seeds and membranes. Turn tomatoes upside down to drain on paper towel-lined plate or baking sheet.

2. Combine mayonnaise, garlic and lemon juice in medium bowl; mix well. Add crabmeat, olives, almonds and pepper; stir gently to blend.

3. Spoon crab mixture into tomatoes. Serve immediately.

MAKES 8 TO 10 SERVINGS

TIP: For the best flavor, do not refrigerate the stuffed tomatoes. Crab mixture can be prepared several hours in advance and refrigerated. Stuff tomatoes with the crab mixture just before serving.

CHILI PUFFS

1 package (about 17 ounces) frozen puff pastry (2 sheets), thawed

1 can (about 15 ounces) chili without beans

½ (8-ounce) package cream cheese, softened

½ cup (2 ounces) finely shredded sharp Cheddar cheese

Sliced green onions (optional)

1. Preheat oven to 400°F.

2. Roll each sheet of puff pastry into 18×9-inch rectangle on lightly floured surface. Cut each rectangle into 18 (3-inch) squares. Press dough into bottoms and up sides of 36 mini (1¾-inch) muffin cups. Bake 10 minutes.

3. Beat chili and cream cheese in medium bowl until smooth. Fill each pastry shell with 2 teaspoons chili mixture, pressing down centers of pastry to fill, if necessary. Sprinkle with Cheddar cheese.

4. Bake 5 to 7 minutes or until cheese is melted and edges of pastry are golden brown. Cool in pans 5 minutes; remove to wire racks. Garnish with green onions; serve warm.

MAKES 36 PUFFS

TIP: Use a pizza cutter to easily cut puff pastry sheets.

EMPANADITAS

1 tablespoon butter

1 cup finely chopped onion

2 cups finely chopped cooked chicken

¼ cup canned diced green chiles

1 tablespoon capers, drained and coarsely chopped

¼ teaspoon salt

1 cup (4 ounces) shredded Monterey Jack cheese

Pastry for double-crust 9-inch pie

1 egg yolk

1 teaspoon water

1. Preheat oven to 375°F. Melt butter in medium skillet over medium heat. Add onion; cook and stir 3 minutes or until softened. Stir in chicken, chiles, capers and salt; cook and stir 1 minute. Remove from heat; stir in cheese.

2. Roll out pastry, one half at a time, to ⅛-inch thickness on floured surface. Cut out 2½-inch circles with biscuit cutter. Place about 1 teaspoon filling on each circle. Fold dough over filling to make half moons; seal edges with fork. Prick tops with fork to vent.

3. Whisk egg yolk and water in small bowl; brush over dough. Place on ungreased baking sheets.

4. Bake 12 to 15 minutes or until golden brown. Serve warm.

MAKES ABOUT 36 EMPANADITAS

CREAMY MUSHROOM CUPS

2 tablespoons butter

4 ounces mushrooms, coarsely chopped

¼ teaspoon salt

2 cloves garlic, minced

2 tablespoons dry sherry

¼ cup whipping cream

15 frozen mini phyllo shells, thawed and heated according to package directions

¼ cup chopped fresh parsley

1. Melt butter in large nonstick skillet over medium heat. Add mushrooms and salt; cook and stir 3 minutes or until tender. Add garlic; cook and stir 15 seconds.

2. Stir in sherry until blended. Stir in cream; cook and stir 2 minutes or until thickened.

3. Divide mushroom mixture evenly among phyllo shells. Sprinkle with parsley; serve immediately.

MAKES 5 SERVINGS

SHRIMP RAMEN EGG ROLLS

1 tablespoon vegetable oil

8 ounces small raw shrimp, peeled, deveined and coarsely chopped

1 cup diced red bell pepper

1 package (3 ounces) shrimp-flavored ramen noodles

2 tablespoons chopped green onion

10 egg roll wrappers

Additional vegetable oil for frying

Sweet and sour sauce

1. Heat 1 tablespoon oil in large skillet over medium-high heat. Add shrimp and bell pepper; cook and stir 5 minutes or until shrimp are pink and opaque and bell pepper is softened. Transfer to large bowl.

2. Break noodles into large chunks; set seasoning packet aside. Cook noodles according to package directions; drain and rinse under cold running water to stop cooking. Add noodles to bowl with shrimp. Stir in reserved seasoning packet and green onion; mix well.

3. Place one egg roll wrapper on work surface with one corner facing you. Place 2 tablespoons filling across center. Fold bottom and sides in over filling; roll up. Moisten edge with water to seal. Repeat with remaining wrappers and filling.

4. Heat 1 inch oil in large skillet to 350°F. Cook egg rolls in batches about 2 minutes per side or until golden brown. Drain on paper towel-lined plate. Serve with sweet and sour sauce.

MAKES 10 EGG ROLLS

VARIATION: Egg rolls may be baked instead of fried. Brush tops of egg rolls lightly with vegetable oil; bake in preheated 375°F oven 15 minutes or until crisp.

SPINACH CHEESE BUNDLES

1 package (6½ ounces) garlic-
  and-herb spreadable cheese
½ cup packed chopped fresh
  spinach

¼ teaspoon black pepper
1 package (about 17 ounces) frozen
  puff pastry (2 sheets), thawed
Sweet and sour sauce (optional)

1. Preheat oven to 400°F. Combine cheese, spinach and pepper in small bowl; mix well.

2. Roll out each sheet of puff pastry into 12-inch square on lightly floured surface. Cut each square into 16 (3-inch) squares.

3. Place about 1 teaspoon cheese mixture in center of each square. Brush edges of squares with water. Bring edges together over filling; twist tightly to seal. Fan out corners of puff pastry. Place bundles 2 inches apart on ungreased baking sheets.

4. Bake about 13 minutes or until golden brown. Serve warm with sweet and sour sauce, if desired.

MAKES 32 BUNDLES

SMALL PLATES

SAUSAGE AND KALE
STUFFED MINI PIZZAS

1 tablespoon olive oil

4 ounces spicy turkey or pork Italian sausage

⅓ cup finely chopped red onion

2½ cups packed chopped stemmed kale

¼ teaspoon salt

1 loaf (16 ounces) frozen pizza dough or white bread dough, thawed according to package directions

¾ cup (3 ounces) shredded Italian blend cheese

¼ cup pizza sauce

1. Preheat oven to 400°F. Spray 12 standard (2½-inch) muffin pan cups with nonstick cooking spray.

2. Heat oil in large skillet over medium-high heat. (If using pork sausage, oil is not needed.) Remove sausage from casings; crumble into skillet. Cook and stir about 5 minutes or until no longer pink. Remove to plate. Add onion to skillet; cook and stir 4 minutes or until softened. Add kale; cook about 10 minutes or until tender, stirring occasionally. Return sausage to skillet with salt; stir until blended. Set aside to cool slightly.

3. Divide dough into 12 pieces. Stretch or roll each piece into 5-inch circle; press into prepared muffin cups. Sprinkle 1 teaspoon cheese into bottom of each cup; spread 1 teaspoon pizza sauce over cheese. Top evenly with kale mixture and remaining cheese.

4. Bake about 16 minutes or until golden brown. Let stand in pan 1 minute; loosen sides with small spatula or knife. Remove to wire rack. Serve warm.

MAKES 12 MINI PIZZAS

STEAMED PORK WONTONS

DIPPING SAUCE

2 tablespoons sugar
2 tablespoons white vinegar
2 tablespoons lime juice
2 tablespoons soy sauce

WONTONS

8 ounces ground pork
¼ cup chopped fresh cilantro

1½ tablespoons grated fresh ginger
1 teaspoon grated orange peel
¼ teaspoon ground red pepper
⅛ teaspoon salt
24 wonton wrappers
3 teaspoons vegetable oil
1 cup water

1. For sauce, combine sugar, vinegar, lime juice and soy sauce in small bowl; mix well.

2. Combine pork, cilantro, ginger, orange peel, red pepper and salt in medium bowl; mix well. Working with one wonton wrapper at a time, place rounded teaspoon pork mixture in center of wrapper. Moisten edges with water and bring corners together; twist to seal.

3. Heat 1½ teaspoons oil in large nonstick skillet over medium-high heat. Add 12 wontons; cook 1 minute or until bottoms are golden brown. Add ½ cup water; cover and cook 5 minutes or until water has evaporated. Remove to platter; tent with foil to keep warm. Repeat with remaining oil, wontons and water.

4. If desired, microwave sauce on HIGH 20 to 30 seconds. Serve wontons with sauce.

MAKES 24 WONTONS

CORN AND BLACK BEAN STUFFED TORTILLA CUPS

3 tablespoons vegetable oil, divided

1 teaspoon salt, divided

½ teaspoon chili powder

6 (6-inch) flour tortillas

1 cup corn

1 cup chopped red bell pepper

1 cup canned black beans, rinsed and drained

1 small ripe avocado, diced

¼ cup lime juice

¼ cup chopped fresh cilantro

1 small jalapeño pepper, seeded and minced

1. Preheat oven to 350°F. Spray six standard (2½-inch) muffin cups with nonstick cooking spray. Combine 1 tablespoon oil, ½ teaspoon salt and chili powder in small bowl; mix well.

2. Stack tortillas; wrap loosely in waxed paper. Microwave on HIGH 10 to 15 seconds or just until softened. Brush one side of each tortilla lightly with oil mixture; press into prepared muffin cups, oiled side up.

3. Bake about 10 minutes or until edges are golden brown. Cool in pan 2 minutes; remove to wire rack to cool completely.

4. Combine corn, bell pepper, beans and avocado in large bowl. Whisk remaining 2 tablespoons oil, ½ teaspoon salt, lime juice, cilantro and jalapeño in small bowl until well blended. Add to corn mixture; toss gently to coat. Fill tortilla cups with salad. Serve immediately. (Tortilla cups and corn salad can be prepared ahead of time; fill cups just before serving.)

MAKES 6 CUPS

TIP: For slightly larger tortilla cups, use the back of the muffin pan instead. Spray the back of a 12-cup muffin pan with nonstick cooking spray. Soften the tortillas and brush with the oil mixture as directed in step 2, then fit them between the cups on the back of the muffin pan. (Only about 3 will fit at one time, so two batches are required.) Bake at 350°F about 8 minutes or until the edges are golden brown.

SHORTCUT POTATO AND CHEESE PIEROGI

2 tablespoons butter

1 large onion, chopped

1½ teaspoons salt, divided

1 pound baking potatoes, peeled and cut into 1-inch pieces

⅛ teaspoon black pepper

1 cup (4 ounces) shredded fontina, gruyère or white Cheddar cheese

⅓ cup grated Parmesan cheese

40 to 50 round pot sticker or gyoza wrappers*

4½ to 6 tablespoons vegetable oil, divided

1½ to 2 cups water, divided

Fresh herbs and red pepper flakes (optional)

If only square wrappers are available, cut out circles with biscuit cutter or cut ½-inch triangle off all corners of wrappers to make rounded shapes.

1. Melt butter in large skillet over medium-high heat. Add onion and ¼ teaspoon salt; cook and stir 5 minutes or until onion begins to brown. Reduce heat to medium-low; cook 20 minutes or until onion is deep golden brown, stirring occasionally.

2. Meanwhile, place potatoes in medium saucepan; add 1 teaspoon salt and water to cover by 2 inches. Bring to a boil over medium heat; cook about 10 minutes or until potatoes are tender.

3. Drain potatoes; transfer to medium bowl and mash until smooth. Add caramelized onion, remaining ¼ teaspoon salt and pepper; mix well. Stir in cheeses until blended.

4. Line baking sheet with parchment paper or waxed paper. Place wrappers, one at a time, on clean work surface. Place 2 teaspoons potato filling in center of wrapper. Lightly moisten edges with water; fold wrappers in half over filling. Press edges together to seal, crimping or pleating as desired. Place on prepared baking sheet. Keep finished pierogi covered with plastic wrap while filling remaining wrappers.

5. Heat 1½ tablespoons oil in large nonstick skillet over medium-high heat. Arrange pierogi in single layer in skillet (do not crowd); cook 2 minutes or until bottoms are golden brown. Turn and cook 2 minutes. Add ½ cup water to skillet; cover and cook 2 to 3 minutes or until pierogi are tender and water has evaporated. Repeat with remaining oil, pierogi and water. Garnish as desired.

MAKES 6 TO 8 SERVINGS

CHIPOTLE CHICKEN STUFFED QUESADILLAS

1 package (8 ounces) cream cheese, softened

1 cup (4 ounces) shredded Mexican cheese blend

1 tablespoon minced canned chipotle pepper in adobo sauce

5 (10-inch) flour tortillas

5 cups shredded cooked chicken (about 1¼ pounds)

Optional toppings: guacamole, sour cream, salsa and chopped fresh cilantro

1. Combine cream cheese, Mexican cheese blend and chipotle pepper in large bowl; mix well.

2. Spread ⅓ cup cheese mixture over half of one tortilla. Top with about 1 cup chicken; fold tortilla over filling and press gently. Repeat with remaining tortillas, cheese mixture and chicken.

3. Heat large nonstick skillet over medium-high heat. Spray outside surface of each quesadilla with nonstick cooking spray. Cook quesadillas 2 to 3 minutes per side or until lightly browned.

4. Cut quesadillas into wedges. Serve with desired toppings.

MAKES 5 SERVINGS

LOBSTER POT STICKERS

4 dried black Chinese mushrooms

¼ cup plus 2 teaspoons soy sauce, divided

3 teaspoons dark sesame oil, divided

1 tablespoon rice vinegar

8 ounces lobster-flavored surimi, finely chopped

2 cups chopped napa or green cabbage

¼ cup chopped green onions

1 tablespoon minced fresh ginger

26 round wonton wrappers*

2 tablespoons vegetable oil, divided

1 cup chicken broth, divided

If only square wrappers are available, cut out circles with biscuit cutter or cut ½-inch triangle off all corners of wrappers to make rounded shapes.

1. Place mushrooms in medium bowl; cover with warm water. Let stand 20 to 40 minutes or until softened.

2. Meanwhile, combine ¼ cup soy sauce, 1 teaspoon sesame oil and rice vinegar in small bowl; mix well.

3. Drain mushrooms; discard water. Cut off and discard stems. Chop caps; return to bowl. Add lobster, cabbage, green onions, ginger, remaining 2 teaspoons soy sauce and 2 teaspoons sesame oil; stir gently until blended.

4. Place wonton wrappers on work surface. Working in batches, place about 2 teaspoons lobster mixture in center of each wrapper. Lightly moisten edges with water; fold wrappers in half over filling. Press edges together to seal. Keep finished potstickers covered with plastic wrap while filling remaining wrappers.

5. Heat 1 tablespoon vegetable oil in large nonstick skillet over medium heat. Add half of pot stickers; cook 2 to 3 minutes per side or until golden brown.

6. Pour ½ cup broth into skillet. Reduce heat to low; cover and cook 10 minutes or until all liquid is absorbed. Repeat with remaining vegetable oil, pot stickers and broth. Serve immediately with sauce for dipping.

MAKES 26 POT STICKERS

TIP: Pot stickers may be cooked immediately or covered tightly and refrigerated up to 4 hours or frozen up to 3 months. To freeze, place pot stickers on baking sheet; place in freezer 30 minutes to firm slightly. Transfer to freezer food storage bag. (Frozen pot stickers do not need to be thawed before cooking.)

MICRO MINI STUFFED POTATOES

1 **pound small new red potatoes**	½ **teaspoon salt**
¼ **cup sour cream**	¼ **teaspoon black pepper**
2 **tablespoons butter, softened**	¼ **cup finely chopped green onions (optional)**
½ **teaspoon minced garlic**	
¼ **cup milk**	
½ **cup (2 ounces) shredded sharp Cheddar cheese**	

MICROWAVE DIRECTIONS

1. Pierce potatoes with fork in several places. Microwave potatoes on HIGH 5 to 6 minutes or until tender. Let stand 5 minutes; cut in half lengthwise. Scoop out pulp from potatoes; set potato shells aside.

2. Beat potato pulp in medium bowl with electric mixer at low speed 30 seconds. Add sour cream, butter and garlic; beat until well blended. Gradually add milk, beating until smooth. Add cheese, salt and pepper; beat until blended.

3. Fill potato shells evenly with potato mixture. Microwave on HIGH 1 to 2 minutes or until cheese is melted. Garnish with green onions.

MAKES 4 SERVINGS

SPICY BEEF TURNOVERS

8 ounces ground beef or turkey

2 cloves garlic, minced

2 tablespoons soy sauce

1 tablespoon water

½ teaspoon cornstarch

1 teaspoon curry powder

¼ teaspoon Chinese five-spice powder

¼ teaspoon red pepper flakes

2 tablespoons minced green onion

1 package (7½ ounces) refrigerated buttermilk biscuits (10 biscuits)

1 egg

1 tablespoon water

1. Preheat oven to 400°F. Line baking sheet with parchment paper or spray with nonstick cooking spray.

2. Cook beef and garlic in medium skillet over medium-high heat until beef is no longer pink, stirring to break up meat. Drain fat.

3. Stir soy sauce and water into cornstarch in small bowl until smooth. Add soy sauce mixture, curry powder, five-spice powder and red pepper flakes to skillet; cook and stir 30 seconds or until liquid is absorbed. Remove from heat; stir in green onion.

4. Separate biscuits; roll each biscuit into 4-inch round between two sheets of waxed paper. Spoon heaping tablespoon beef mixture onto one side of each biscuit; fold dough over filling to form semicircle. Pinch edges together to seal. Place turnovers on prepared baking sheet. Beat egg and water in small bowl; brush lightly over turnovers.

5. Bake 9 to 10 minutes or until golden brown. Serve warm or at room temperature.

MAKES 10 TURNOVERS

TIP: The turnovers may be wrapped before baking and frozen up to 3 months. Thaw completely before proceeding with baking as directed in step 5.

VEGETARIAN SUMMER ROLLS

1 package (14 ounces) firm tofu, drained

3½ ounces thin rice noodles (rice vermicelli)

½ cup soy sauce, divided

2 tablespoons lime juice

1 tablespoon sugar

2 cloves garlic, crushed

1 teaspoon rice vinegar

1 teaspoon dark sesame oil

1 tablespoon vegetable oil

2 medium portobello mushrooms, cut into thin strips

1 tablespoon sesame seeds

12 rice paper wrappers*

1 bunch fresh mint

½ cup shredded carrots

1 yellow bell pepper, cut into thin strips

Rice papers are thin, edible wrappers used in Southeast Asian cooking, available at Asian markets or the Asian section of many supermarkets.

1. Cut tofu crosswise into two pieces, each about 1 inch thick. Place between paper-towel lined cutting boards. Place weighted saucepan or baking dish on top; let stand 30 minutes to drain.

2. Place rice noodles in medium bowl; cover with hot water. Soak 20 to 30 minutes or until softened. Drain and cut into 3-inch lengths.

3. Meanwhile, prepare dipping sauce. Combine ¼ cup soy sauce, lime juice, sugar, garlic and vinegar in small bowl; stir until sugar is dissolved. Set aside.

4. Cut tofu into thin strips (about ¼ inch); place in medium bowl. Add remaining ¼ cup soy sauce and sesame oil; toss gently to coat. Heat vegetable oil in large skillet over medium heat. Add tofu and mushrooms; cook and stir until browned. Sprinkle with sesame seeds.

5. Soften rice paper wrappers, one at a time, in bowl of warm water 20 to 30 seconds. Place on flat surface lined with clean kitchen towel. Arrange mint leaves in center of wrapper. Layer with tofu, mushrooms, carrots, noodles and bell pepper.

6. Fold bottom of wrapper up over filling; fold in sides and roll up. Repeat with remaining wrappers. Wrap finished rolls individually in plastic wrap or cover with damp towel until ready to serve to prevent drying out. Serve with dipping sauce.

MAKES 12 SUMMER ROLLS

SPANIKOPITA CUPS

6 tablespoons (¾ stick) butter, melted

2 eggs

1 container (15 ounces) ricotta cheese

1 package (10 ounces) frozen chopped spinach, thawed and squeezed dry

1 package (4 to 5 ounces) crumbled feta cheese

¾ teaspoon finely grated lemon peel

½ teaspoon salt

¼ teaspoon black pepper

⅛ teaspoon ground nutmeg

8 sheets frozen phyllo dough, thawed

1. Preheat oven to 350°F. Brush 16 standard (2½-inch) muffin pan cups with some of butter.

2. Whisk eggs in large bowl. Add ricotta, spinach, feta, lemon peel, salt, pepper and nutmeg; whisk until well blended.

3. Place one sheet of phyllo on work surface. Brush with some of butter; top with second sheet. Repeat layers twice. Cut stack of phyllo into eight rectangles; fit rectangles into prepared muffin cups, pressing into bottoms and up sides of cups. Repeat with remaining four sheets of phyllo and butter. Fill phyllo cups with spinach mixture.

4. Bake about 18 minutes or until phyllo is golden brown and filling is set. Cool in pans 2 minutes; remove to wire racks. Serve warm.

MAKES 16 CUPS

DIM SUM BAKED BUNS

6 to 8 dried shiitake mushrooms

3 green onions, minced

2 tablespoons prepared plum sauce

1 tablespoon hoisin sauce

1 tablespoon vegetable oil

8 ounces ground chicken

4 cloves garlic, minced

1 tablespoon minced fresh ginger

8 frozen bread dough rolls (about 18 ounces total), thawed according to package directions

1 egg, beaten

¾ teaspoon sesame seeds

1. Place mushrooms in medium bowl; cover with warm water. Let stand 30 minutes or until softened. Line two baking sheets with parchment paper or spray with nonstick cooking spray.

2. Rinse mushrooms well; drain and squeeze out excess water. Cut off and discard stems. Finely chop caps; return to bowl. Stir in green onions, plum sauce and hoisin sauce; mix well.

3. Heat oil in medium nonstick skillet over high heat. Add chicken; cook without stirring 1 to 2 minutes or until no longer pink. Add garlic and ginger; cook and stir 2 minutes. Stir in mushroom mixture.

4. Lightly flour hands and work surface. Cut rolls in half; roll each half into a ball. Shape each piece between hands to form disk. Press edge of disk between thumb and forefinger, working in circular motion to form circle 3 to 3½ inches in diameter (center of disk should be thicker than edges.) Place disks on work surface. Place 1 generous tablespoon filling in center of each disk. Lift edge of dough up and around filling; pinch edges together to seal. Place seam side down on prepared baking sheets. Cover and let rise in warm place 45 minutes or until doubled in size. Preheat oven to 375°F.

5. Brush buns with egg; sprinkle with sesame seeds. Bake 16 to 18 minutes or until golden brown.

MAKES 16 BUNS

APRICOT BRIE EN CROÛTE

1 sheet frozen puff pastry (half of 17-ounce package)

1 round Brie cheese (8 ounces)
¼ cup apricot preserves

1. Unfold puff pastry; thaw 20 minutes on lightly floured surface. Preheat oven to 400°F. Line baking sheet with parchment paper.

2. Roll out puff pastry into 12-inch square. Place cheese in center of square; spread preserves over top of cheese.

3. Gather up edges of puff pastry; bring together over center of cheese, covering completely. Pinch and twist pastry edges together to seal. Transfer to prepared baking sheet.

4. Bake 20 to 25 minutes or until golden brown. (If top of pastry browns too quickly, cover loosely with small piece of foil.) Serve warm.

MAKES 6 SERVINGS

VARIATION: For added flavor and texture, sprinkle 2 tablespoons sliced almonds over the preserves. Proceed with wrapping and baking as directed.

PEPPERONI AND CHEESE STUFFED BREAD

1 package (about 14 ounces) refrigerated pizza dough

8 slices provolone cheese

20 to 30 slices pepperoni (about half of 6-ounce package)

½ teaspoon Italian seasoning

¾ cup (3 ounces) shredded mozzarella cheese

½ cup grated Parmesan cheese

1 egg, beaten

Marinara sauce, heated

1. Preheat oven to 400°F. Unroll pizza dough on sheet of parchment paper with long side in front of you. Cut off corners of dough to create oval shape.

2. Arrange half of provolone slices over bottom half of oval, cutting to fit as necessary. Top with pepperoni; sprinkle with ¼ teaspoon Italian seasoning. Top with mozzarella, Parmesan and remaining provolone slices; sprinkle with remaining ¼ teaspoon Italian seasoning.

3. Fold top half of dough over filling to create half moon (calzone) shape; press edges with fork or pinch edges to seal. Transfer calzone with parchment paper to large baking sheet; curve slightly into crescent shape. Brush with beaten egg.

4. Bake about 16 minutes or until crust is golden brown. Remove to wire rack to cool slightly. Cut crosswise into slices; serve warm with marinara sauce.

MAKES ABOUT 6 SERVINGS

BAKED EGG ROLLS

Sesame Dipping Sauce (page 83)

1 ounce dried shiitake mushrooms

1 large carrot, shredded

1 can (8 ounces) sliced water chestnuts, drained and minced

3 green onions, minced

3 tablespoons chopped fresh cilantro

2 tablespoons vegetable oil, divided

12 ounces ground chicken

2 tablespoons minced fresh ginger

6 cloves garlic, minced

2 tablespoons soy sauce

2 teaspoons water

1 teaspoon cornstarch

12 egg roll wrappers

1 teaspoon sesame seeds

1. Prepare Sesame Dipping Sauce; set aside.

2. Place mushrooms in medium bowl; cover with warm water. Let stand 30 minutes or until softened. Rinse well; drain and squeeze out excess water. Cut off and discard stems. Finely chop caps; return to bowl. Stir in carrot, water chestnuts, green onions and cilantro; mix well.

3. Heat 1 tablespoon oil in medium nonstick skillet over medium-high heat. Cook chicken 2 minutes, stirring to break up meat. Add ginger and garlic; cook and stir 2 minutes or until chicken is cooked through. Add to mushroom mixture. Sprinkle with soy sauce; mix well.

4. Preheat oven to 425°F. Spray baking sheet with nonstick cooking spray. Stir water into cornstarch in small bowl until smooth. Place one wrapper on work surface. Spoon about ⅓ cup filling across center of wrapper to within about ½ inch of sides. Fold bottom of wrapper over filling; fold in sides. Brush ½-inch strip across top edge with cornstarch mixture; roll up and seal securely. Place rolls seam side down on baking sheet. Repeat with remaining wrappers. Brush egg rolls with remaining 1 tablespoon oil; sprinkle with sesame seeds.

5. Bake 18 minutes or until golden brown and crisp. Serve with dipping sauce.

MAKES 12 EGG ROLLS

SESAME DIPPING SAUCE: Combine ¼ cup rice vinegar, 4 teaspoons soy sauce, 2 teaspoons minced fresh ginger and 1 teaspoon dark sesame oil in small bowl; mix well.

LUNCH

CHICKEN, HUMMUS AND VEGETABLE STUFFED WRAPS

¾ **cup hummus (regular, roasted red pepper or roasted garlic)**

4 **(8- to 10-inch) sun-dried tomato or spinach wraps *or* whole wheat tortillas**

2 **cups chopped cooked chicken breast**

Chipotle hot pepper sauce or Louisiana-style hot pepper sauce (optional)

½ **cup shredded carrots**

½ **cup chopped unpeeled cucumber**

½ **cup thinly sliced radishes**

2 **tablespoons chopped fresh mint *or* basil**

1. Spread hummus evenly over wraps all the way to edges.

2. Arrange chicken over hummus; sprinkle with hot pepper sauce, if desired. Top with carrots, cucumber, radishes and mint.

3. Roll up wraps and filling tightly. Cut in half diagonally.

MAKES 4 SERVINGS

VARIATION: Cut the wraps into bite-size pieces for a quick and easy appetizer.

HAWAIIAN PIZZA ROLLS

2 tablespoons cornmeal, divided

1 package (about 14 ounces) refrigerated pizza dough

6 ounces thinly sliced Canadian bacon

1/3 cup crushed pineapple, drained

1/3 cup pizza sauce, plus additional for serving

3 pieces (1 ounce each) string cheese

1. Preheat oven to 400°F. Line baking sheet with parchment paper or spray with nonstick cooking spray. Sprinkle with 1 tablespoon cornmeal.

2. Roll out dough into 16½×11-inch rectangle on lightly floured surface. Sprinkle with remaining 1 tablespoon cornmeal. Cut into six squares. Top squares with bacon, pineapple and 1/3 cup pizza sauce.

3. Cut each piece of string cheese in half; place 1 piece of cheese in center of each square. Bring up opposite sides of each square and seal. Crimp ends of rolls to seal. Place rolls, seam side down, on prepared baking sheet.

4. Bake 15 to 17 minutes or until golden brown. Serve warm, room temperature or chilled with additional pizza sauce for dipping.

MAKES 6 SERVINGS

STUFFED TURKEY PITAS

½ cup whole berry cranberry sauce

2 to 3 tablespoons coarse grain mustard

8 ounces chopped cooked turkey breast (about 1 cup)

4 pita bread rounds, cut in half crosswise

4 cups packed spring greens (about 3½ ounces)

½ cup thinly sliced red onion

½ cup crumbled blue cheese

1. Combine cranberry sauce and mustard in medium bowl; mix well. Add turkey; stir to coat.

2. Fill each pita half evenly with greens, turkey mixture, onion and cheese. Serve immediately.

MAKES 4 SERVINGS

CHICKEN FAJITA ROLL-UPS

1 cup ranch dressing

1 teaspoon chili powder

2 tablespoons vegetable oil, divided

2 teaspoons lime juice

2 teaspoons fajita seasoning mix

½ teaspoon chipotle chili powder

¼ teaspoon salt

4 boneless skinless chicken breasts (about 6 ounces each)

4 (8- to 9-inch) flour tortillas

1 cup (4 ounces) shredded Cheddar cheese

1 cup (4 ounces) shredded Monterey Jack cheese

3 cups shredded lettuce

1 cup pico de gallo

1. Combine ranch dressing and chili powder in small bowl; mix well. Refrigerate until ready to serve.

2. Combine 1 tablespoon oil, lime juice, fajita seasoning mix, chipotle chili powder and salt in small bowl; mix well. Coat both sides of chicken with spice mixture.

3. Heat remaining 1 tablespoon oil in large nonstick skillet or grill pan over medium-high heat. Add chicken; cook about 5 minutes per side or until cooked through. Remove to plate; let stand 5 minutes before slicing. Cut chicken breasts in half lengthwise, then cut crosswise into ½-inch strips.

4. Wipe out skillet with paper towel. Place one tortilla in skillet; sprinkle with ¼ cup Cheddar and ¼ cup Monterey Jack. Heat over medium heat until cheeses are melted. Remove tortilla to work surface or cutting board.

5. Sprinkle ¾ cup shredded lettuce down center of one tortilla; top with ¼ cup pico de gallo and one fourth of chicken. Fold bottom of tortilla up over filling, then fold in sides and roll up. Cut in half diagonally. Repeat with remaining tortillas, cheese and fillings. Serve with ranch dipping sauce.

MAKES 4 SERVINGS

HAM AND CHEESE STUFFED QUESADILLAS

1 tablespoon vegetable oil

1 cup thinly sliced red onion

1 small jalapeño pepper, seeded and minced*

1 cup pitted fresh sweet cherries

1 tablespoon packed brown sugar

1 teaspoon balsamic vinegar

¼ teaspoon salt

3 ounces ham, thinly sliced

2 ounces Havarti cheese, thinly sliced

2 (8- to 9-inch) flour tortillas

2 teaspoons butter

Jalapeño peppers can sting and irritate the skin, so wear rubber gloves when handling peppers and do not touch your eyes.

1. Heat oil in large skillet over medium-high heat. Add onion and jalapeño; cook and stir 4 minutes or until onions are golden. Add cherries; cook and stir 1 minute. Stir in brown sugar, vinegar and salt; cook over low heat 1 minute, stirring constantly. Remove from heat; set jam aside to cool slightly.

2. Arrange half of ham slices and half of cheese slices over one side of each tortilla. Top with one fourth of cherry jam. Fold tortillas in half. Set aside remaining jam.

3. Melt butter in skillet over medium heat. Add quesadillas; press down firmly with spatula. Cook 3 to 4 minutes per side or until cheese is melted and quesadillas are golden brown. Cut quesadillas in half; serve with remaining cherry jam.

MAKES 2 SERVINGS

VEGETABLE STUFFED CRESCENT ROLLS

2 tablespoons butter

½ cup diced onion

½ cup diced red bell pepper

½ cup finely chopped mushrooms

½ cup broccoli florets

½ cup beer

¼ teaspoon salt

¼ teaspoon black pepper

1 package (8 ounces) refrigerated crescent roll dough

½ cup (2 ounces) shredded Cheddar cheese

1. Melt butter in medium skillet over medium heat. Add onion and bell pepper; cook and stir 3 minutes or until vegetables are softened. Add mushrooms, broccoli, beer, salt and black pepper; cook 5 minutes or until beer has evaporated. Remove from heat; set aside to cool to room temperature.

2. Preheat oven to 375°F. Separate crescent roll dough into eight pieces. Sprinkle about 1 tablespoon cheese on wide end of one piece of dough; top with 1 tablespoon vegetable mixture. Starting with wide end, roll up dough and filling; seal point closed and curve roll into crescent shape. Place on ungreased baking sheet. Repeat with remaining dough, cheese and filling.

3. Bake 11 to 13 minutes or until rolls are golden brown. Serve warm.

MAKES 8 SERVINGS

ROAST BEEF WRAPS

½ cup whipped cream cheese

2 tablespoons mayonnaise

1 to 2 teaspoons prepared horseradish

Salt and black pepper

4 (8-inch) flour tortillas

4 green leaf lettuce leaves

½ red onion, thinly sliced

½ pound deli sliced roast beef

1 tomato, thinly sliced

1. Combine cream cheese, mayonnaise and horseradish in small bowl; mix well. Season with salt and pepper. Wrap tortillas in paper towels; microwave on HIGH 20 seconds to soften slightly.

2. Spread one fourth of cream cheese mixture over each tortilla, leaving 1-inch border. Top with lettuce, onion, roast beef and tomato.

3. Roll up tortillas; wrap in plastic wrap and refrigerate 30 minutes. Cut in half to serve.

MAKES 4 SERVINGS

GREEK STUFFED PITAS

½ cup plain yogurt

1 medium clove garlic, minced

½ teaspoon dried oregano

4 whole wheat pita rounds, cut in half crosswise

4 cups (4 ounces) packed spring greens

½ medium cucumber, peeled and chopped

½ cup thinly sliced red onion

2 cups diced cooked chicken

1 cup chopped tomato

1 ounce peperoncinis, stemmed and chopped

¼ cup (1 ounce) crumbled feta cheese

1. Combine yogurt, garlic and oregano in small bowl; mix well.

2. Fill each pita half evenly with greens, cucumber and onion; top with chicken, tomato, peperoncinis and cheese. Serve with yogurt sauce.

MAKES 4 SERVINGS

HAM AND CHEESE FILLED BISCUITS

1 package (12 ounces) refrigerated flaky buttermilk biscuits (10 biscuits)

½ cup finely chopped red bell pepper

⅓ cup diced ham

2 tablespoons mayonnaise

1 tablespoon Dijon mustard

¾ cup (3 ounces) finely shredded sharp Cheddar cheese

1. Preheat oven to 400°F. Line baking sheet with parchment paper or spray with nonstick cooking spray.

2. Split each biscuit in half to make 20 rounds. Arrange 10 rounds in single layer on prepared baking sheet.

3. Combine bell pepper, ham, mayonnaise and mustard in medium bowl; mix well. Stir in cheese. Mound equal amounts in center of 10 biscuit rounds. Cover with remaining rounds, stretching gently to cover mixture completely. Press edges together to enclose filling and seal.

4. Bake 11 to 12 minutes or until biscuits are golden brown. Let stand 5 minutes before serving.

MAKES 10 SERVINGS

SPINACH VEGGIE WRAPS

PICO DE GALLO

- 1 cup finely chopped tomatoes (about 2 small)
- ½ teaspoon salt
- ¼ cup chopped white onion
- 2 tablespoons minced jalapeno pepper*
- 2 tablespoons chopped fresh cilantro
- 1 teaspoon lime juice

GUACAMOLE

- 2 large ripe avocados
- ¼ cup finely chopped red onion
- 2 tablespoons chopped fresh cilantro
- 2 teaspoons fresh lime juice
- ½ teaspoon salt

WRAPS

- 4 (10-inch) whole wheat tortillas
- 2 cups fresh baby spinach leaves
- 1 cup sliced mushrooms
- 1 cup shredded Asiago cheese
  Salsa

Jalapeño peppers can sting and irritate the skin, so wear rubber gloves when handling peppers and do not touch your eyes.

1. For pico de gallo, combine tomatoes and ½ teaspoon salt in fine-mesh strainer; set over bowl to drain 15 minutes. Combine drained tomatoes, white onion, jalapeño, 2 tablespoons cilantro and 1 teaspoon lime juice in medium bowl; mix well.

2. For guacamole, combine avocados, red onion, 2 tablespoons cilantro, 2 teaspoons lime juice and ½ teaspoon salt in medium bowl; mash with fork to desired consistency.

3. For wraps, spread ¼ cup guacamole on each tortilla. Layer each with ½ cup spinach, ¼ cup mushrooms, ¼ cup cheese and ¼ cup pico de gallo. Roll up; serve with salsa.

MAKES 4 SERVINGS

CHICKEN BACON STUFFED QUESADILLAS

4 teaspoons vegetable oil, divided

4 (8-inch) flour tortillas

1 cup (4 ounces) shredded Colby-Jack cheese

2 cups coarsely chopped cooked chicken

4 slices bacon, crisp-cooked, coarsely chopped

½ cup pico de gallo, plus additional for serving

Sour cream and guacamole (optional)

1. Heat large nonstick skillet over medium heat; brush with 1 teaspoon oil. Place one tortilla in skillet; sprinkle with ¼ cup cheese. Spread ½ cup chicken over one half of tortilla; top with one fourth of bacon and 2 tablespoons pico de gallo.

2. Cook 1 to 2 minutes or until cheese is melted and bottom of tortilla is lightly browned. Fold tortilla over filling, pressing with spatula. Transfer to cutting board; cool slightly. Cut into wedges. Repeat with remaining ingredients. Serve with additional pico de gallo, sour cream and guacamole, if desired.

MAKES 4 SERVINGS

BEAN AND PEPPER STUFFED BURRITOS

2 teaspoons canola oil

1½ cups diced red, yellow and green bell peppers *or* 1 large green bell pepper, diced

½ cup chopped onion

1 can (about 15 ounces) black beans, rinsed and drained

½ cup salsa

1 teaspoon chili powder

7 (8-inch) flour tortillas, warmed

¾ cup (3 ounces) shredded Cheddar or Mexican cheese blend

½ cup chopped fresh cilantro

1. Heat oil in large nonstick skillet over medium heat. Add bell peppers and onion; cook and stir 3 to 4 minutes. Stir in beans, salsa and chili powder; cook and stir 5 to 8 minutes or until vegetables are tender and sauce is thickened.

2. Spoon about ⅔ cup bean mixture down center of each tortilla; top with cheese and cilantro. Roll up to enclose filling.

MAKES 7 SERVINGS

SANDWICH MONSTERS

1 package (about 16 ounces) refrigerated jumbo buttermilk biscuits (8 biscuits)

1 cup (4 ounces) shredded mozzarella cheese

⅓ cup sliced mushrooms

2 ounces pepperoni slices (about 35 slices), quartered

½ cup pizza sauce, plus additional for serving

1 egg, beaten

1. Preheat oven to 350°F. Line baking sheet with parchment paper or foil.

2. Separate biscuits; set aside one biscuit for decoration. Roll out remaining biscuits into 7-inch rounds on lightly floured surface.

3. Top half of each round evenly with cheese, mushrooms, pepperoni and ⅓ cup pizza sauce, leaving ½-inch border. Fold dough over filling to form semicircle; seal edges with fork. Brush tops with egg.

4. Split remaining biscuit horizontally; cut each half into eight ¼-inch strips. For each sandwich, roll two strips of dough into spirals for eyes. Divide remaining two strips of dough into seven pieces for noses. Arrange eyes and noses on tops of sandwiches; brush with egg. Place on prepared baking sheet.

5. Bake 20 to 25 minutes or until crust is golden brown. Remove to wire rack; cool 5 minutes. Serve with additional pizza sauce.

MAKES 7 SERVINGS

BUFFALO CHICKEN STUFFED WRAPS

4 boneless skinless chicken breasts (4 to 6 ounces each)

¼ cup plus 2 tablespoons buffalo wing sauce, divided

2 cups broccoli slaw

1 tablespoon blue cheese salad dressing

4 (8-inch) whole wheat tortillas, warmed

1. Place chicken in large resealable food storage bag. Add ¼ cup buffalo sauce; seal bag and turn to coat. Marinate in refrigerator 15 minutes.

2. Heat grill pan or large skillet over medium-high heat. Cook chicken 5 to 6 minutes per side or until no longer pink in center. Remove to plate; set aside until cool enough to handle. Cut chicken into ½-inch slices. Combine chicken and remaining 2 tablespoons buffalo sauce in medium bowl; stir to coat.

3. Combine broccoli slaw and blue cheese dressing in medium bowl; mix well.

4. Layer chicken and broccoli slaw evenly down center of each tortilla. Roll up to enclose filling. To serve, cut in half diagonally.

MAKES 4 SERVINGS

VARIATION: Substitute your favorite barbecue sauce for the buffalo wing sauce.

DINNER

BLUE CHEESE STUFFED CHICKEN BREASTS

½ **cup crumbled blue cheese**

2 **tablespoons butter, softened, divided**

¾ **teaspoon dried thyme**

Salt and black pepper

4 **bone-in skin-on chicken breasts**

1 **tablespoon lemon juice**

1. Preheat oven to 400°F. Combine cheese, 1 tablespoon butter and thyme in small bowl; mix well. Season with salt and pepper.

2. Loosen chicken skin by pushing fingers between skin and meat, taking care not to tear skin. Spread cheese mixture under skin; massage skin to spread mixture evenly over chicken breasts. Place in shallow roasting pan.

3. Melt remaining 1 tablespoon butter in small bowl; stir in lemon juice until blended. Brush mixture over chicken. Sprinkle with salt and pepper.

4. Roast 50 minutes or until chicken is cooked through (165°F).

MAKES 4 SERVINGS

HOMEMADE SPINACH RAVIOLI

1 package (10 ounces) frozen
  chopped spinach, thawed
  and squeezed dry

1 cup ricotta cheese

½ cup grated Romano or Parmesan
  cheese

1 egg

1 tablespoon minced fresh basil

½ teaspoon salt

½ teaspoon black pepper

¼ teaspoon ground nutmeg

36 round wonton wrappers*

1 jar (about 26 ounces) marinara
  or other pasta sauce

*If only square wrappers are available,
cut out circles with biscuit cutter or
cut ½-inch triangle off all corners of
wrappers to make rounded shapes.*

1. Combine spinach, cheeses, egg, basil, salt, pepper and nutmeg in medium bowl; mix well. (Filling may be prepared up to 1 day in advance and refrigerated.)

2. Place two wonton wrappers on lightly floured surface, keeping remaining wrappers covered. Place 1 heaping teaspoon filling in center of each wrapper. Moisten edges around filling; top with second wrapper. Press edges gently around filling to remove air bubbles and seal. Repeat with remaining wrappers and filling.

3. Bring large pot of salted water to a boil. Meanwhile, heat marinara sauce in medium saucepan over low heat. Add half of ravioli to boiling water; stir gently and cook over medium-high heat about 3 minutes or until ravioli rise to surface. Remove ravioli to platter with slotted spoon; keep warm. Repeat with remaining ravioli. Serve with marinara sauce.

MAKES ABOUT 4 SERVINGS

GRILLED SALMON STUFFED QUESADILLAS

1 medium cucumber, peeled, seeded and finely chopped

½ cup green or red salsa

1 salmon fillet (8 ounces)

3 tablespoons olive oil, divided

4 (10-inch) flour tortillas, warmed

6 ounces goat cheese, crumbled *or* 1½ cups (6 ounces) shredded Monterey Jack cheese

¼ cup drained pickled jalapeño pepper slices

1. Prepare grill for direct cooking. Combine cucumber and salsa in small bowl; set aside. Brush salmon with 2 tablespoons oil.

2. Grill salmon, covered, over medium-high heat 5 to 6 minutes per side or until fish begins to flake when tested with fork. Remove to plate; flake with fork.

3. Spread salmon evenly over half of each tortilla, leaving 1-inch border. Sprinkle with cheese and jalapeño slices. Fold tortillas in half over filling; brush with remaining 1 tablespoon oil.

4. Grill quesadillas over medium-high heat about 2 minutes or until browned on both sides and cheese is melted. Serve with salsa mixture.

MAKES 4 SERVINGS

BELL PEPPER AND RICOTTA STUFFED CALZONES

1 tablespoon olive oil

1 medium red bell pepper, diced

1 medium green bell pepper, diced

1 small onion, diced

½ teaspoon Italian seasoning

⅛ teaspoon black pepper

1 clove garlic, minced

1¼ cups marinara sauce, divided

¼ cup ricotta cheese

¼ cup (1 ounce) mozzarella cheese

1 container (about 14 ounces) refrigerated pizza dough

1. Preheat oven to 375°F. Line baking sheet with parchment paper or spray with nonstick cooking spray.

2. Heat oil in large nonstick skillet over medium heat. Add bell peppers, onion, Italian seasoning and black pepper; cook about 8 minutes or until vegetables are tender, stirring occasionally. Add garlic; cook and stir 1 minute. Stir in ½ cup marinara sauce; cook about 2 minutes or until thickened slightly. Transfer to plate; set aside to cool slightly.

3. Combine ricotta and mozzarella in small bowl; mix well. Unroll dough on work surface; cut into six 4-inch squares. Pat each square into 5-inch square. Spoon ⅓ cup vegetable mixture into center of each square; sprinkle with 1 tablespoon cheese mixture. Fold dough over filling to form triangle; pinch and fold edges together to seal. Transfer calzones to prepared baking sheet.

4. Bake 15 to 18 minutes or until calzones are lightly browned. Remove to wire rack to cool 5 minutes; serve warm with remaining marinara sauce.

MAKES 6 SERVINGS

SPINACH STUFFED MANICOTTI

8 uncooked manicotti pasta shells
1 tablespoon olive oil
1 teaspoon dried rosemary
1 teaspoon dried sage
1 teaspoon dried oregano
1 teaspoon dried thyme
1 teaspoon minced garlic

1½ cups chopped fresh tomatoes
1 package (10 ounces) frozen spinach, thawed and squeezed dry
½ cup ricotta cheese
½ cup fresh whole wheat bread crumbs
2 egg whites, lightly beaten

1. Cook pasta according to package directions, drain and rinse under cold running water until cool enough to handle.

2. Preheat oven to 350°F. Heat oil in medium saucepan over medium heat. Add rosemary, sage, oregano, thyme and garlic; cook and stir 1 minute. Stir in tomatoes; cook over low heat 10 minutes, stirring occasionally.

3. Combine spinach, cheese and bread crumbs in medium bowl; mix well. Fold in egg whites until blended. Fill manicotti shells with spinach mixture.

4. Pour one third of tomato mixture into 13×9-inch baking dish. Arrange manicotti in dish; top with remaining tomato mixture. Cover with foil.

5. Bake 30 minutes or until hot and bubbly.

MAKES 4 SERVINGS

PECAN AND APPLE STUFFED PORK CHOPS

4 thick-cut bone-in pork loin chops
(about 12 ounces each)

1 teaspoon salt, divided

½ teaspoon black pepper, divided

2 tablespoons vegetable oil

½ cup diced green apple

½ small onion, minced

¼ teaspoon dried thyme

½ cup apple brandy or brandy

⅔ cup bread cubes

2 tablespoons chopped pecans

4 tablespoons (½ stick) frozen
butter

1 cup apple juice

SLOW COOKER DIRECTIONS

1. Season pork chops with ½ teaspoon salt and ¼ teaspoon pepper. Heat oil in large skillet over medium-high heat. Add pork in batches, if necessary; cook 2 minutes per side or until browned.

2. Add apple, onion, thyme, remaining ½ teaspoon salt and remaining ¼ teaspoon pepper to skillet; cook and stir over medium heat 3 minutes or until onion is translucent. Remove from heat; pour in brandy. Return skillet to medium heat; cook until most of liquid is absorbed. Stir in bread and pecans; cook and stir 1 minute.

3. Cut each pork chop horizontally to form pocket; place 1 tablespoon butter in each pocket. Divide stuffing evenly among pork chops. Arrange pork chops in slow cooker, pocket side up. Pour apple juice around pork chops.

4. Cover; cook on HIGH 1½ to 1¾ hours or until pork is 145°F.

MAKES 4 SERVINGS

BBQ CHICKEN STROMBOLI

1 **rotisserie-roasted chicken***
   (2 to 2¼ pounds)

⅓ **cup barbecue sauce**

1 **package (about 14 ounces)**
   refrigerated pizza dough

1 **cup (4 ounces) shredded Cheddar**
   cheese

⅓ **cup sliced green onions, divided**

Or use 8 ounces deli roast chicken
breast, chopped, instead of the
2 cups shredded rotisserie chicken.

1. Remove and discard chicken skin. Shred chicken meat; discard bones. (You should have about 4 cups shredded chicken.) Combine 2 cups chicken and barbecue sauce in medium bowl; stir to coat. Cover and refrigerate or freeze remaining chicken for another use.

2. Preheat oven to 400°F. Line baking sheet with parchment paper or spray with nonstick cooking spray. Unroll dough on baking sheet; pat into 12×9-inch rectangle.

3. Spread chicken mixture lengthwise down center of dough, leaving 2½ inches on each side. Sprinkle with cheese and ¼ cup green onions. Fold long sides of dough over filling; press edges to seal. Sprinkle with remaining green onions.

4. Bake 19 to 22 minutes or until golden brown. Let stand 10 minutes before slicing.

MAKES 6 SERVINGS

PICADILLO STUFFED TACOS

6 ounces ground beef

½ cup chopped green bell pepper

½ teaspoon ground cumin

½ teaspoon chili powder

⅛ teaspoon ground cinnamon

½ cup chunky salsa

1 tablespoon golden raisins

4 (6-inch) flour or corn tortillas, warmed

½ cup shredded lettuce

¼ cup (1 ounce) shredded Cheddar cheese

1 small tomato, chopped

1. Combine beef, bell pepper, cumin, chili powder and cinnamon in large nonstick skillet; cook and stir over medium heat until beef is browned.

2. Stir in salsa and raisins; cook over low heat 5 minutes or until beef is cooked through, stirring occasionally.

3. Divide beef mixture evenly among tortillas. Top with lettuce, cheese and tomato.

MAKES 2 SERVINGS

STUFFED CHICKEN FLORENTINE

4 large boneless skinless chicken breasts (6 to 8 ounces each)

1 cup shredded Asiago or mozzarella cheese

½ cup thawed well-drained frozen chopped spinach

2 tablespoons chopped fresh basil

⅛ teaspoon ground nutmeg

8 to 12 wooden toothpicks, soaked in water

½ teaspoon salt

¼ teaspoon black pepper

2 tablespoons olive oil

2 cloves garlic, minced

2 cups tomato-basil or marinara pasta sauce

1. Preheat oven to 375°F. Use sharp knife to cut horizontal slit in side of each chicken breast half to form pocket.

2. Combine cheese, spinach, basil and nutmeg in medium bowl; mix well. Stuff mixture into pockets; close with toothpicks. Sprinkle chicken with salt and pepper.

3. Heat oil in large ovenproof skillet over medium heat. Add chicken; cook 3 minutes or until lightly browned. Turn chicken; add garlic to skillet and cook 3 minutes. Pour pasta sauce over and around chicken.

4. Transfer skillet to oven; bake 12 to 14 minutes or until chicken is no longer pink in center.

MAKES 4 SERVINGS

BACON AND BLUE CHEESE STUFFED BURGERS

4 slices bacon	1½ pounds ground beef
1 small red onion, finely chopped	Salt and black pepper
2 tablespoons crumbled blue cheese	4 onion or plain hamburger rolls
1 tablespoon butter, softened	Lettuce leaves

1. Cook bacon in large skillet over medium-high heat until almost crisp. Drain on paper towel-lined plate. Finely chop bacon; place in small bowl. Add onion to same skillet; cook and stir 4 minutes or until softened. Add to bowl with bacon; set aside to cool slightly. Stir in cheese and butter until well blended.

2. Prepare grill for direct cooking.

3. Divide beef into eight equal portions. Flatten into thin 4-inch patties; season with salt and pepper. Place 2 tablespoons bacon mixture in center of each of four patties; cover with remaining patties. Pinch edges together to seal.

4. Grill patties, covered, over medium-high heat 4 to 5 minutes per side for medium (160°F) Remove to plate; let stand 2 minutes before serving. Serve burgers on rolls with lettuce.

MAKES 4 SERVINGS

TIP: For juicier burgers, do not flatten the patties while cooking. Pressing down on the patties with a spatula not only squeezes out the juices, but may also cause the stuffing to pop out.

PUMPKIN RAVIOLI

½ cup canned pumpkin

¼ teaspoon salt

¼ teaspoon black pepper

1 package (14 ounces) round wonton wrappers*

Whole Italian parsley leaves

2 tablespoons extra virgin olive oil

2 tablespoons butter

2 to 3 cloves garlic, minced

¾ cup shredded Parmesan cheese

2 tablespoons chopped walnuts

If only square wrappers are available, cut out circles with biscuit cutter or cut ½-inch triangle off all corners of wrappers to make rounded shapes.

1. Combine pumpkin, salt and pepper in medium bowl; mix well. Place small bowl of water on work surface.

2. Unwrap wontons; cover with plastic wrap. Place four wontons in a row on work surface. Brush two wontons with water; place one parsley leaf in center of each wonton. Place another wonton over each parsley leaf, pressing out air and sealing edges. Brush one layered wonton with water; place 1 teaspoon pumpkin mixture in center of wonton. Top with remaining layered wonton, pressing out air and sealing edges. Repeat with remaining wontons, parsley leaves and pumpkin filling.

3. Bring large saucepan of salted water to a boil. Working in small batches, slide ravioli into boiling water; cook 1 minute or until ravioli float to surface. Drain ravioli; cover until ready to serve.

4. Heat oil in large skillet over medium-low heat. Add butter and garlic; cook and stir 1 minute or until garlic is fragrant. Add ravioli; cook over low heat 1 minute or until heated through. Sprinkle with cheese and walnuts; serve immediately.

MAKES 4 SERVINGS

EASY MOO SHU PORK

1	tablespoon vegetable oil	1½	cups packaged coleslaw mix
8	ounces pork tenderloin, sliced	2	tablespoons hoisin sauce or Asian plum sauce
4	green onions, cut into ½-inch pieces	4	(8-inch) flour tortillas, warmed

1. Heat oil in large nonstick skillet over medium-high heat. Add pork and green onions; cook and stir 2 to 3 minutes or until pork is barely pink in center. Stir in coleslaw mix and hoisin sauce.

2. Spoon pork mixture onto tortillas. Roll up tortillas, folding in sides to enclose filling.

MAKES 2 SERVINGS

TIP: To warm tortillas, stack and wrap loosely in plastic wrap. Microwave on HIGH 15 to 20 seconds or until hot and pliable.

SPINACH AND RICOTTA STUFFED SHELLS

1 package (16 ounces) jumbo pasta shells

1 container (15 ounces) ricotta cheese

8 ounces frozen chopped spinach, thawed and squeezed dry

½ cup grated Parmesan cheese

1 egg, lightly beaten

1 clove garlic, minced

½ teaspoon salt

1 jar (24 to 26 ounces) marinara pasta sauce

½ cup (2 ounces) shredded mozzarella cheese

1 teaspoon olive oil

SLOW COOKER DIRECTIONS

1. Cook pasta shells according to package directions until almost tender; drain well. Combine ricotta, spinach, Parmesan, egg, garlic and salt in large bowl; mix well.

2. Pour ¼ cup pasta sauce into slow cooker. Spoon 2 to 3 tablespoons ricotta mixture into 1 pasta shell; place in bottom of slow cooker. Repeat with enough additional shells to cover bottom of slow cooker. Top with ¼ cup pasta sauce. Repeat with remaining pasta shells and filling. Top with any remaining pasta sauce; sprinkle with mozzarella. Drizzle with oil.

3. Cover; cook on HIGH 3 to 4 hours or until mozzarella is melted and sauce is hot and bubbly.

MAKES 4 TO 6 SERVINGS

TIP: To cook the shells in the oven instead of the slow cooker, preheat oven to 350°F and spray a 2- to 3-quart baking dish with nonstick cooking spray. Prepare and fill the shells as directed. Spread a thin layer of pasta sauce on the bottom of the prepared baking dish; arrange the filled shells over the sauce and top with the remaining sauce and cheese. Cover with foil and bake 30 minutes or until hot and bubbly.

KALE AND MUSHROOM STUFFED CHICKEN BREASTS

2 tablespoons olive oil, divided
1 cup coarsely chopped mushrooms
2 cups thinly sliced kale
1 tablespoon fresh lemon juice
½ teaspoon salt, divided

4 boneless skinless chicken breasts (about 4 ounces each)
¼ cup crumbled feta cheese
¼ teaspoon black pepper

1. Heat 1 tablespoon oil in large skillet over medium-high heat. Add mushrooms; cook and stir 5 minutes or until mushrooms begin to brown. Add kale; cook and stir 8 minutes or until wilted. Sprinkle with lemon juice and ¼ teaspoon salt. Remove to small bowl; let stand 5 to 10 minutes to cool slightly.

2. Meanwhile, place each chicken breast between sheets of plastic wrap; pound to ½-inch thickness with meat mallet or rolling pin.

3. Gently stir cheese into mushroom mixture. Spoon ¼ cup mixture down center of each chicken breast. Roll up to enclose filling; secure with toothpicks. Sprinkle with remaining ¼ teaspoon salt and pepper.

4. Wipe out same skillet with paper towels. Add remaining 1 tablespoon oil to skillet; heat over medium heat. Add chicken; cook until browned on both sides. Cover and cook 5 minutes per side or until no longer pink. Remove toothpicks before serving.

MAKES 4 SERVINGS

VEGETABLES

CAPRESE STUFFED ZUCCHINI BOATS

3 medium zucchini

1 package (3 ounces) ramen noodles, any flavor, broken into small pieces*

1 tomato, finely chopped

½ cup (2 ounces) shredded mozzarella cheese

2 tablespoons fresh chopped basil

1 tablespoon olive oil

1 clove garlic, minced

½ teaspoon salt

Discard seasoning packet.

1. Preheat oven to 375°F. Cut zucchini in half lengthwise. Scoop out seeds, leaving ½- to ¼-inch shells. Place in 2-quart baking dish.

2. Cook noodles in boiling water 2 minutes; drain and place in large bowl. Stir in tomato, cheese, basil, oil, garlic and salt; mix well. Divide mixture among zucchini shells.

3. Bake 25 minutes or until zucchini and noodles are lightly browned.

MAKES 6 SERVINGS

STUFFED BABY BELL PEPPERS

1 tablespoon olive oil

½ medium onion, chopped

½ pound ground beef, chicken or turkey

½ cup cooked white rice

3 tablespoons chopped fresh parsley

2 tablespoons lemon juice

1 tablespoon dried dill weed

1 tablespoon tomato paste, divided

½ teaspoon salt

⅛ teaspoon black pepper

1 package yellow and red baby bell peppers (about 24)

¼ cup vegetable, chicken or beef broth

SLOW COOKER DIRECTIONS

1. Heat oil in medium skillet over medium heat. Add onion; cook and stir 4 minutes or until translucent.

2. Add beef; cook until browned, stirring to break up meat. Drain fat. Transfer to large bowl; stir in rice, parsley, lemon juice, dill weed, 1½ teaspoons tomato paste, salt and black pepper until well blended.

3. Cut small slit in the side of each baby bell pepper; run under cold running water to remove seeds. Fill each pepper with 2 to 3 teaspoons beef mixture. Place peppers in slow cooker, slit side up. Add broth and remaining tomato paste.

4. Cover; cook on LOW 5 hours or on HIGH 2½ hours. Serve hot.

MAKES 6 TO 8 SERVINGS

MIDDLE EASTERN STUFFED SQUASH

4 **medium to large yellow squash**
1 **tablespoon olive oil**
12 **ounces ground turkey**
1 **teaspoon ground cinnamon**
½ **cup finely chopped onion**
1 **ounce pine nuts, toasted***
1 **teaspoon sugar**
¾ **teaspoon salt**

¼ **teaspoon ground cumin**
⅛ **teaspoon ground red pepper**
½ **cup plain yogurt**
2 **tablespoons chopped fresh mint**

* To toast pine nuts, cook in medium skillet over medium heat 2 minutes or until lightly browned, stirring frequently.

1. Preheat oven to 350°F. Cut squash into halves lengthwise. Scrape out inner pulp and seeds, leaving ½-inch shell. Chop pulp; set aside.

2. Heat oil in large nonstick skillet over medium-high heat. Add turkey and cinnamon; cook until turkey is no longer pink, stirring to break up meat. Remove to plate.

3. Add onion and chopped squash to skillet; cook and stir 4 minutes or until squash is tender. Remove from heat; stir in turkey mixture, pine nuts, sugar, salt, cumin and red pepper; mix well. Arrange squash halves, cut sides up, in 13×9-inch baking pan. Spoon turkey mixture into squash halves. Cover with foil.

4. Bake 30 to 45 minutes or until squash is tender.

5. Meanwhile, combine yogurt and mint in small bowl; mix well. Refrigerate until ready to serve. Serve squash with yogurt sauce.

MAKES 4 SERVINGS

CURRIED TUNA STUFFED TOMATOES

4 medium ripe tomatoes
1 can (12 ounces) water-packed tuna, drained and flaked
¼ cup diced Granny Smith apple
¼ cup diced red onion

¼ cup mayonnaise
3 tablespoons golden raisins
1¼ teaspoons curry powder
¼ teaspoon salt

1. Cut off about ½ inch from stem end of tomatoes; hollow out insides.

2. Combine tuna, apple, onion, mayonnaise, raisins, curry powder and salt in medium bowl; stir gently until blended.

3. Fill tomatoes evenly with tuna mixture.

MAKES 4 SERVINGS

SIMPLE STUFFED SQUASH

¼ **cup raisins**

2 **acorn squash (about 4 inches in diameter)**

2 **tablespoons butter, melted**

2 **tablespoons sugar**

¼ **teaspoon ground cinnamon**

2 **tablespoons butter**

2 **medium Fuji apples, cut into ½-inch pieces**

1. Place raisins in small bowl; cover with warm water. Let stand 20 minutes. Preheat oven to 375°F.

2. Cut acorn squash into quarters; remove seeds. Place squash in 13×9-inch baking dish; drizzle with melted butter. Combine sugar and cinnamon in small bowl; sprinkle squash with half of cinnamon mixture.

3. Bake squash 10 minutes. Meanwhile, melt 2 tablespoons butter in small saucepan over medium heat. Drain raisins; add to saucepan with apples and remaining cinnamon mixture. Cook and stir 1 minute. Top partially baked squash with apple mixture.

4. Bake 30 to 35 minutes or until apples and squash are tender. Serve warm.

MAKES 8 SERVINGS

PEPPERS STUFFED WITH YELLOW SQUASH AND RICE

½ cup uncooked long grain brown rice

5 large green, red or yellow bell peppers, divided

2 teaspoons olive oil

2 medium yellow squash (1 pound), chopped

1 small onion, diced

2 cloves garlic, minced

1 large tomato, chopped

½ cup tomato sauce

½ cup grated Parmesan cheese

3 tablespoons chopped fresh parsley

¼ teaspoon salt

⅛ teaspoon black pepper

1. Cook rice according to package directions. Preheat oven to 400°F. Spray 13×9-inch baking dish with nonstick cooking spray.

2. Bring large saucepan of water to a boil. Cut tops off 4 bell peppers; scrape out seeds and membranes. Place bell peppers in boiling water; cook 4 minutes to soften slightly. Drain peppers; set aside.

3. Chop remaining bell pepper. Heat oil in large nonstick skillet over medium-high heat. Add chopped bell pepper, squash and onion; cook about 5 minutes or until vegetables are softened, stirring frequently. Add garlic; cook and stir 1 minute. Add cooked rice, tomato and tomato sauce; cook until heated through. Stir in cheese, parsley, salt and black pepper.

4. Fill each bell pepper with about ½ cup rice mixture. Arrange stuffed peppers in single layer in prepared baking dish.

5. Bake, uncovered, 25 to 30 minutes or until peppers are heated through.

MAKES 4 SERVINGS

PIZZA STUFFED POTATOES

4 medium potatoes (about
    7 ounces each)

¾ cup pizza sauce

⅛ teaspoon garlic powder

2 teaspoons grated Parmesan
    cheese

1 ounce pepperoni slices
    (about 16), quartered

¾ cup (3 ounces) shredded
    mozzarella cheese

MICROWAVE DIRECTIONS

1. Pierce potatoes with fork; microwave on HIGH 5 to 7 minutes or until soft. Split potatoes open with knife; mash insides lightly.

2. Top each potato with 3 tablespoons pizza sauce; mix gently into potato. Sprinkle with garlic powder and Parmesan; top with pepperoni and mozzarella.

3. Return potatoes to microwave; cook on HIGH 1 minute or until cheese is melted.

MAKES 4 SERVINGS

STUFFED WINTER SQUASH
WITH ARTICHOKES

4 small yellow winter squash
(about 8 ounces each),
cut in half lengthwise

1 tablespoon olive oil

¾ cup finely chopped onion

¾ teaspoon dried oregano

1½ cups cooked brown or white rice

1 jar (12 ounces) marinated
artichoke hearts, drained
and coarsely chopped

¾ cup canned navy beans, rinsed
and drained

⅓ cup mayonnaise

¼ cup grated Parmesan cheese

¼ cup chopped fresh parsley

½ teaspoon salt

¼ teaspoon garlic powder

¼ teaspoon Italian seasoning

1 cup (4 ounces) shredded
mozzarella cheese

1. Preheat oven to 350°F. Remove seeds and flesh from each squash half; coarsely chop flesh. Set aside shells.

2. Heat oil in large skillet over medium-high heat. Add chopped squash, onion and oregano; cook and stir 4 minutes or until onion is translucent.

3. Remove from heat; stir in rice, artichokes, beans, mayonnaise, Parmesan, parsley, salt, garlic powder and Italian seasoning; mix well. Divide mixture evenly among squash shells. Place on baking sheet.

4. Bake 40 minutes or until shells are tender. Sprinkle with mozzarella; bake 3 minutes or until cheese is melted.

MAKES 4 SERVINGS

VARIATION: Substitute 2 large squash, about 1 pound each, for 4 smaller squash. Cut squash in half lengthwise, then cut each half in half crosswise.

SAVORY STUFFED ONIONS

4 medium onions (2 to 2½ pounds, 3 inches in diameter)

4 ounces bulk pork sausage

1½ cups packed baby spinach, coarsely chopped

2 tablespoons half-and-half

⅓ cup shredded Monterey Jack or pizza blend cheese, plus additional for garnish

2 tablespoons dry bread crumbs

1 tablespoon butter, melted

1. Fill large saucepan two-thirds full of water. Bring to a boil over high heat.

2. Meanwhile, cut 1-inch slice off top of each onion. Peel onions but do not cut off root end. Score center layers of onion with thin-bladed serrated knife. Carefully twist knife and remove centers of onions, leaving at least three outer layers. Discard centers or reserve for another use. *Do not cut all the way through root end.* Insert skewers through one side of each onion.

3. Place onions in boiling water. Reduce heat to low; cook 15 minutes. Remove onions from water, invert onto plate and cool 15 minutes. Cut thin slice from root end of each onion. Remove skewers. If openings in onions are less than 1½ inches wide, remove additional inner layers. Preheat oven to 350°F. Line 9-inch baking dish with foil.

4. Cook sausage in small skillet over medium heat until browned, stirring occasionally. Add spinach and half-and-half; cover and cook 2 minutes or until spinach is wilted, stirring once. Remove from heat; stir in ⅓ cup cheese until melted. Stir in bread crumbs. Transfer to medium bowl; set aside to cool slightly.

5. Place onions in prepared baking dish. Divide sausage filling among onions, piling any extra on top. Cover with foil.

6. Bake 15 minutes. Remove foil; brush onions with melted butter. Bake 10 to 15 minutes or until onions reach desired tenderness. Sprinkle with additional cheese, if desired.

MAKES 4 SERVINGS

SPINACH AND FETA FARRO STUFFED PEPPERS

1 tablespoon olive oil

1 package (about 5 ounces) baby spinach

½ cup sliced green onions

2 cloves garlic, crushed

1 tablespoon chopped fresh oregano

1 package (8½ ounces) quick-cooking farro, prepared according to package directions using vegetable broth instead of water

1 can (about 14 ounces) petite diced tomatoes, drained

⅛ teaspoon black pepper

1 container (4 ounces) crumbled feta cheese, divided

3 large bell peppers, halved lengthwise, seeds and membranes removed

1. Preheat oven to 350°F.

2. Heat oil in large skillet over medium-high heat. Add spinach, green onions, garlic and oregano; cook and stir 3 minutes. Stir in farro, tomatoes, black pepper and ½ cup cheese; mix well.

3. Spoon farro mixture into bell pepper halves (about ¾ cup each); place in shallow baking pan. Pour ¼ cup water into bottom of pan; cover with foil.

4. Bake 30 minutes or until bell peppers are crisp-tender and filling is heated through. Sprinkle with remaining cheese.

MAKES 6 SERVINGS

BARLEY AND PEAR STUFFED ACORN SQUASH

3 small acorn or carnival squash

2 cups vegetable broth

¾ teaspoon salt, divided

1 cup uncooked quick-cooking barley

2 tablespoons butter

1 small onion, chopped

1 stalk celery, chopped

¼ teaspoon black pepper

1 large unpeeled ripe pear, diced

½ cup chopped hazelnuts, toasted*

¼ cup maple syrup

½ teaspoon ground cinnamon

*To toast hazelnuts, spread on ungreased baking sheet. Bake at 350°F 7 to 10 minutes or until light golden brown, stirring occasionally.

1. Preheat oven to 350°F. Pierce squash with knife in several places. Microwave on HIGH 8 to 10 minutes or until tender, turning once. Let stand 5 minutes.

2. Meanwhile, combine broth and ½ teaspoon salt in large saucepan; bring to a boil over high heat. Stir in barley. Reduce heat to low; cover and cook 12 minutes or until tender. (Do not drain.)

3. Cut squash in half lengthwise; scoop out and discard seeds. Arrange squash halves, cut sides up, in large baking dish.

4. Melt butter in large skillet over medium heat. Add onion, celery, remaining ¼ teaspoon salt and pepper; cook and stir 5 minutes. Add pear; cook 5 minutes. Stir in barley, hazelnuts, maple syrup and cinnamon until well blended. Spoon barley mixture into squash halves. Cover with foil.

5. Bake 15 to 20 minutes or until heated through.

MAKES 6 SERVINGS

BARLEY AND APPLE STUFFED ACORN SQUASH: Substitute 1 apple for the pear and walnuts for the hazelnuts.

NOTE: Squash can be stuffed ahead of time. Prepare as directed and bake at 350°F 25 to 30 minutes or until heated through.

BLACK BEAN AND RICE STUFFED POBLANO PEPPERS

2 large *or* 4 small poblano peppers

½ (15-ounce) can black beans, rinsed and drained

½ cup cooked brown rice

⅓ cup mild or medium chunky salsa

⅓ cup shredded Cheddar cheese or pepper Jack cheese, divided

¼ teaspoon salt

1. Preheat oven to 375°F. Spray shallow baking pan with nonstick cooking spray.

2. Cut thin slice from one side of each pepper. Chop pepper slices; set aside. Bring medium saucepan two-thirds full of water to a boil over medium heat. Add peppers; cook 6 minutes. Drain peppers; rinse under cold running water. Remove and discard seeds and membranes.

3. Combine beans, rice, salsa, chopped pepper, ¼ cup cheese and salt in medium bowl; mix well. Spoon into peppers, mounding mixture. Place peppers in prepared pan. Cover with foil.

4. Bake 12 to 15 minutes or until heated through. Sprinkle with remaining cheese; bake 2 minutes or until cheese is melted.

MAKES 2 SERVINGS

DESSERTS

CHERRY TURNOVERS

1 can (21 ounces) cherry pie filling
2 teaspoons grated orange peel
1 package (about 15 ounces)
   refrigerated pie crusts (2 crusts)

1 egg yolk
1 tablespoon milk
1 tablespoon sugar
½ teaspoon ground cinnamon

1. Preheat oven to 375°F. Combine pie filling and orange peel in medium bowl; mix well.

2. Roll out one pie crust into 12-inch circle on lightly floured surface. Cut out six 4-inch rounds with cookie cutter. Repeat with second crust.

3. Beat egg yolk and milk in small bowl until blended. Combine sugar and cinnamon in separate small bowl.

4. Spoon scant tablespoon pie filling mixture in center of each pastry round. Brush edges with egg yolk mixture; fold in half to enclose filling. Press edges together with fork to seal. Place on ungreased baking sheet. Cut slits in tops of turnovers with paring knife. Brush with remaining egg yolk mixture; sprinkle with cinnamon-sugar.

5. Bake 18 to 20 minutes or until golden brown. Remove to wire rack; cool slightly. Serve warm.

MAKES 12 TURNOVERS

CHOCOLATE SPRING ROLLS

½ cup whipping cream

2 tablespoons butter

6 ounces semisweet or bittersweet chocolate, chopped

½ cup chopped peanuts

12 egg roll wrappers

Water

Vegetable oil for frying

Powdered sugar (optional)

1. Combine cream and butter in small saucepan; bring to a boil over medium-high heat. Remove from heat; sprinkle chocolate over cream mixture. Let stand 1 minute; whisk until smooth. Stir in peanuts. Refrigerate 1 hour or until firm.

2. Working with one egg roll wrapper at a time, place wrapper on work surface. Spoon 1 rounded tablespoon chocolate filling in center of wrapper, shaping chocolate into elongated shape. Brush edges of wrapper with water. Fold in sides; roll up very tightly. Cover with plastic wrap while making remaining spring rolls.

3. Heat ¾ inch oil in large skillet over medium heat to 350°F. Fry spring rolls in small batches about 1 minute per side or until golden brown. Remove to paper towel-lined plate with slotted spoon. Sprinkle with powdered sugar just before serving, if desired.

MAKES 12 SPRING ROLLS

CANDY CALZONES

1 **package small chocolate, peanut
   and nougat candy bars,
   chocolate peanut butter cups
   or other chocolate candy bar
   (8 bars)**

1 **package (about 15 ounces)
   refrigerated pie crusts
   (2 crusts)**
½ **cup milk chocolate chips**

1. Preheat oven to 375°F. Line baking sheet with parchment paper. Chop candy into ¼-inch pieces.

2. Unroll pie crusts on cutting board or clean work surface. Cut out 3-inch circles with biscuit cutter. Place about 1 tablespoon chopped candy on one side of each circle; fold dough over candy to form semicircle. Crimp edges with fingers or fork to seal. Place on prepared baking sheet.

3. Bake about 12 minutes or until crust is golden brown. Remove to wire rack to cool slightly.

4. Place chocolate chips in small microwavable bowl; microwave on HIGH 1 minute. Stir; microwave at 30-second intervals until smooth. Drizzle melted chocolate over calzones; serve warm.

MAKES 16 CALZONES

RASPBERRY-FILLED CHOCOLATE RAVIOLI

1 cup (2 sticks) butter, softened
½ cup granulated sugar
2 squares (1 ounce each) bittersweet or semisweet chocolate, melted and cooled
1 egg
1 teaspoon vanilla

½ teaspoon chocolate extract
¼ teaspoon baking soda
Dash salt
2½ cups all-purpose flour
1 cup seedless raspberry jam
Powdered sugar

1. Beat butter and granulated sugar in large bowl with electric mixer until blended. Add melted chocolate, egg, vanilla, chocolate extract, baking soda and salt; beat until light. Beat in flour at low speed just until stiff dough forms. Divide dough in half. Wrap each half in plastic wrap; refrigerate until firm.

2. Preheat oven to 350°F. Line cookie sheets with parchment paper or spray with nonstick cooking spray.

3. Roll out dough, half at a time, to ⅛-inch thickness between two sheets of plastic wrap. Remove top sheet of plastic. (If dough gets too soft and sticks to plastic, refrigerate until firm.) Cut dough into 1½-inch squares.

4. Place half of squares 2 inches apart on prepared cookie sheets. Place about ½ teaspoon jam in center of each square; top with second square. Press edges of squares together with fork to seal; pierce center of each square.

5. Bake 10 minutes or just until edges are browned. Remove to wire racks to cool. Dust lightly with powdered sugar.

MAKES ABOUT 6 DOZEN COOKIES

PUMPKIN CHEESECAKE STUFFED PASTRY

1 package frozen puff pastry shells (6 shells)

1 package (4-serving size) vanilla instant pudding and pie filling mix

1 cup milk

1 package (8 ounces) cream cheese, softened

½ (15-ounce) can solid-pack pumpkin

⅓ cup maple syrup

2 teaspoons ground cinnamon, plus additional for garnish

1 teaspoon vanilla

¼ teaspoon ground nutmeg

¼ teaspoon ground allspice

1. Bake puff pastry shells according to package directions. Cool completely.

2. Meanwhile, combine pudding mix, milk, cream cheese, pumpkin, maple syrup, 2 teaspoons cinnamon, vanilla, nutmeg and allspice in food processor; process until smooth. Transfer to medium bowl; cover and refrigerate until ready to serve.

3. Just before serving, remove tops of pastry shells. Spoon about ½ cup pumpkin filling into each shell; garnish with additional cinnamon and tops of pastry shells.

MAKES 6 SERVINGS

CHOCOLATE SURPRISE COOKIES

2¾ cups all-purpose flour

¾ cup unsweetened cocoa powder

½ teaspoon baking powder

½ teaspoon baking soda

1 cup (2 sticks) butter, softened

1½ cups packed brown sugar

½ cup plus 1 tablespoon granulated sugar, divided

2 eggs

1 teaspoon vanilla

1 cup chopped pecans, divided

1 package (9 ounces) caramels coated in milk chocolate

3 squares (1 ounce each) white chocolate, coarsely chopped

1. Preheat oven to 375°F. Combine flour, cocoa, baking powder and baking soda in medium bowl; mix well.

2. Beat butter, brown sugar and ½ cup granulated sugar with electric mixer at medium speed until light and fluffy. Beat in eggs and vanilla until blended. Gradually add flour mixture and ½ cup pecans; beat just until blended. Cover and refrigerate 15 minutes or until dough is firm enough to roll into balls.

3. Combine remaining ½ cup pecans and 1 tablespoon granulated sugar in shallow dish. Roll tablespoonful of dough around 1 caramel candy, covering completely. Press one side of dough ball into nut mixture; place on ungreased cookie sheet, nut side up. Repeat with remaining dough and candies, placing 3 inches apart.

4. Bake 10 to 12 minutes or until set and slightly cracked. Cool on cookie sheet 2 minutes; remove to wire racks to cool completely.

5. Place white chocolate in small resealable food storage bag; seal bag. Microwave on MEDIUM (50%) 2 minutes. Turn and microwave 2 to 3 minutes or until melted. Knead bag until chocolate is smooth. Cut off small corner of bag; drizzle chocolate over cookies. Let stand about 30 minutes or until chocolate is set.

MAKES ABOUT 3½ DOZEN COOKIES

PEANUT BUTTER AND JELLY
STUFFED CUPCAKES

1 package (about 15 ounces) yellow cake mix, plus ingredients to prepare mix

2 cups strawberry jelly

¾ cup creamy peanut butter

½ cup (1 stick) butter, softened

2 cups powdered sugar

½ teaspoon vanilla

¼ cup milk

1. Preheat oven to 350°F. Line 22 standard (2½-inch) muffin cups with paper baking cups.

2. Prepare cake mix according to package directions. Spoon batter evenly into prepared muffin cups. Bake 20 minutes or until toothpick inserted into centers comes out clean. Cool in pans 10 minutes; remove to wire racks to cool completely.

3. Place jelly in pastry bag fitted with small round tip. Insert tip into tops of cupcakes; squeeze bag gently to fill centers with jelly.

4. Beat peanut butter and butter in medium bowl with electric mixer at medium speed 2 minutes or until smooth. Add powdered sugar and vanilla; beat at low speed 1 minute or until crumbly. Slowly add milk, beating until creamy. Pipe or spread frosting onto cupcakes.

MAKES 22 CUPCAKES

INDIVIDUAL FRIED APPLE CRANBERRY PIES

3 **tablespoons butter**	¼ **teaspoon ground nutmeg**
3 **Gala apples (about 12 ounces), peeled and diced**	⅛ **teaspoon salt**
3 **tablespoons dried cranberries**	1 **package (about 15 ounces) refrigerated pie crusts (2 crusts)**
3 **tablespoons packed brown sugar**	**Vegetable oil**
1½ **tablespoons lemon juice**	**Powdered sugar**
¾ **teaspoon ground cinnamon**	

1. Melt butter in large skillet over medium heat. Add apples; cook 8 minutes, stirring frequently. Add cranberries, brown sugar, lemon juice, cinnamon, nutmeg and salt; cook and stir 4 minutes or until apples are tender. Transfer to medium bowl; cool 15 minutes.

2. Let crusts stand at room temperature 15 minutes. Heat 2 cups oil in large deep skillet over medium heat to 350°F.

3. Roll out each crust into 12½-inch circle on floured surface; cut out seven 4-inch circles. Place generous tablespoonful apple mixture on half of dough circle, leaving ¼-inch border. Dip finger in water and moisten edge of one dough circle. Fold dough over filling, pressing lightly. Dip fork in flour and crimp edge of dough to seal completely. Repeat with remaining dough and filling.

4. Working in batches, fry pies 1 minute; turn and fry 1 minute or until lightly browned. Transfer pies to paper towel-lined baking sheet. Allow oil temperature to return to 350°F between batches.

5. Sprinkle with powdered sugar; serve warm or at room temperature.

MAKES 14 PIES

NOTE: Granny Smith apples can be substituted for Gala apples. Increase brown sugar to 4 tablespoons and replace lemon juice with water.

VARIATION: Pies can also be baked on a parchment paper-lined baking sheet in a preheated 425°F oven for 10 minutes or until lightly browned.

CHOCOLATE AND PEANUT BUTTER MOLTEN MUG CAKE

¼ cup all-purpose flour

1 tablespoon unsweetened cocoa powder

2 tablespoons sugar

¼ teaspoon baking powder

¼ cup milk

2 tablespoons butter, melted

¼ teaspoon vanilla

1 teaspoon peanut butter

2 teaspoons mini semisweet chocolate chips, divided

MICROWAVE DIRECTIONS

1. Combine flour, cocoa, sugar and baking powder in medium bowl; mix well. Add milk, butter and vanilla; stir until well blended. Pour batter into large microwavable mug or ramekin.

2. Place peanut butter and 1 teaspoon chocolate chips in center of batter; press down slightly.

3. Microwave on HIGH 1 minute. Let stand 10 minutes before serving. Sprinkle with remaining 1 teaspoon chocolate chips.

MAKES 1 SERVING

BACON S'MORE BUNDLES

1¼ cups mini marshmallows

¾ cup semisweet chocolate chips

¾ cup coarsely crushed graham crackers (5 whole graham crackers)

4 slices bacon, crisp-cooked and crumbled

1 package (about 17 ounces) frozen puff pastry (2 sheets), thawed

1. Preheat oven to 400°F. Combine marshmallows, chocolate chips, graham crackers and bacon in medium bowl; mix well.

2. Unfold pastry on lightly floured surface. Roll each pastry sheet into 12-inch square; cut each into four 6-inch squares. Place scant ½ cup marshmallow mixture in center of each square.

3. Brush edges of pastry squares with water. Bring edges together over filling; twist tightly to seal. Place bundles 2 inches apart on ungreased baking sheet.

4. Bake about 20 minutes or until golden brown. Cool on wire rack 5 minutes. Serve warm.

MAKES 4 SERVINGS

CREAM FILLED CUPCAKES

1 **package (about 15 ounces) dark chocolate cake mix, plus ingredients to prepare mix**

½ **cup (1 stick) butter, softened**

¼ **cup shortening**

3 **cups powdered sugar**

1⅓ **cups whipping cream, divided**

1 **teaspoon salt**

2 **cups semisweet chocolate chips**

1. Preheat oven to 350°F. Line 22 standard (2½-inch) muffin cups with paper baking cups.

2. Prepare cake mix according to package directions. Spoon batter evenly into prepared muffin cups. Bake 20 minutes or until toothpick inserted into centers comes out clean. Cool in pans 10 minutes; remove to wire racks to cool completely.

3. Beat butter and shortening in large bowl with electric mixer at medium speed until well blended. Add powdered sugar, ⅓ cup cream and salt; beat at low speed 1 minute. Beat at medium-high speed 2 minutes or until fluffy.

4. Place filling in piping bag fitted with large round tip. Insert tip into tops of cupcakes; squeeze bag gently to fill centers. Reserve remaining filling.

5. Place chocolate chips in medium bowl. Bring remaining 1 cup cream to a simmer in small saucepan over medium heat. Pour cream over chocolate chips; let stand 1 minute. Whisk until chocolate is melted and mixture is smooth.

6. Dip tops of cupcakes in chocolate mixture; place on wire racks. Dip a second time, if desired. Let stand until set. Pipe swirl design on top of chocolate using reserved filling and small round tip.

MAKES 22 CUPCAKES

APPLE PIE POCKETS

2 pieces lavash bread, each cut into 4 rectangles

2 tablespoons melted butter

¾ cup apple pie filling

1 egg, lightly beaten with 1 teaspoon water

½ cup powdered sugar

2½ teaspoons milk

⅛ teaspoon ground cinnamon

1. Preheat oven to 400°F. Line baking sheet with parchment paper.

2. Brush one side of each piece of lavash with butter. Place half of pieces on work surface, buttered-side down. Spoon 3 tablespoons pie filling in center of each lavash, leaving ½-inch border. Brush border with egg mixture. Top with remaining lavash pieces, buttered side up. Press edges together with fork to seal. Use paring knife to cut 3 small slits in center of each pie pocket. Place on prepared baking sheet.

3. Bake 18 minutes or until crust is golden brown and crisp. Remove to wire rack to cool 15 minutes.

4. Combine powdered sugar, milk and cinnamon in small bowl; whisk until smooth. Drizzle glaze over pockets; let stand 15 minutes to set.

MAKES 4 SERVINGS

METRIC CONVERSION CHART

VOLUME MEASUREMENTS (dry)

$\frac{1}{8}$ teaspoon = 0.5 mL
$\frac{1}{4}$ teaspoon = 1 mL
$\frac{1}{2}$ teaspoon = 2 mL
$\frac{3}{4}$ teaspoon = 4 mL
1 teaspoon = 5 mL
1 tablespoon = 15 mL
2 tablespoons = 30 mL
$\frac{1}{4}$ cup = 60 mL
$\frac{1}{3}$ cup = 75 mL
$\frac{1}{2}$ cup = 125 mL
$\frac{2}{3}$ cup = 150 mL
$\frac{3}{4}$ cup = 175 mL
1 cup = 250 mL
2 cups = 1 pint = 500 mL
3 cups = 750 mL
4 cups = 1 quart = 1 L

VOLUME MEASUREMENTS (fluid)

1 fluid ounce (2 tablespoons) = 30 mL
4 fluid ounces ($\frac{1}{2}$ cup) = 125 mL
8 fluid ounces (1 cup) = 250 mL
12 fluid ounces (1$\frac{1}{2}$ cups) = 375 mL
16 fluid ounces (2 cups) = 500 mL

WEIGHTS (mass)

$\frac{1}{2}$ ounce = 15 g
1 ounce = 30 g
3 ounces = 90 g
4 ounces = 120 g
8 ounces = 225 g
10 ounces = 285 g
12 ounces = 360 g
16 ounces = 1 pound = 450 g

DIMENSIONS

$\frac{1}{16}$ inch = 2 mm
$\frac{1}{8}$ inch = 3 mm
$\frac{1}{4}$ inch = 6 mm
$\frac{1}{2}$ inch = 1.5 cm
$\frac{3}{4}$ inch = 2 cm
1 inch = 2.5 cm

OVEN TEMPERATURES

250°F = 120°C
275°F = 140°C
300°F = 150°C
325°F = 160°C
350°F = 180°C
375°F = 190°C
400°F = 200°C
425°F = 220°C
450°F = 230°C

BAKING PAN SIZES

Utensil	Size in Inches/Quarts	Metric Volume	Size in Centimeters
Baking or Cake Pan (square or rectangular)	8×8×2	2 L	20×20×5
	9×9×2	2.5 L	23×23×5
	12×8×2	3 L	30×20×5
	13×9×2	3.5 L	33×23×5
Loaf Pan	8×4×3	1.5 L	20×10×7
	9×5×3	2 L	23×13×7
Round Layer Cake Pan	8×1½	1.2 L	20×4
	9×1½	1.5 L	23×4
Pie Plate	8×1¼	750 mL	20×3
	9×1¼	1 L	23×3
Baking Dish or Casserole	1 quart	1 L	—
	1½ quart	1.5 L	—
	2 quart	2 L	—